Preaching to
SUBURBAN
CAPTIVES

Alvin C. Porteous

Preaching to SUBURBAN CAPTIVES

Alvin C. Porteous

Judson Press ® Valley Forge

PREACHING TO SUBURBAN CAPTIVES

Unless otherwise indicated, Bible quotations in this volume are in accordance with the Revised Standard Version of the Bible, copyrighted 1946, 1952, 1971, 1973 © by the Division of Christian Education of the National Council of the Churches of Christ in the United States of America, and are used by permission.

Other versions of the Bible quoted in this book are:

The Holy Bible, King James Version.

The New English Bible, Copyright © The Delegates of the Oxford University Press and The Syndics of the Cambridge University Press, 1961, 1970.

Today's English Version, the *Good News Bible*—Old Testament: Copyright © American Bible Society 1976; New Testament: Copyright © American Bible Society 1966, 1971, 1976. Used by permission.

The New Testament in Modern English, Rev. Ed., Copyright © J.B. Phillips 1972. Used by permission of The Macmillan Company and Geoffrey Bles, Ltd.

Library of Congress Cataloging in Publication Data
Porteous, Alvin C., 1922-
    Preaching to suburban captives.

    1. Liberation theology. 2. Preaching. 3. Sermons, English. 4. Baptists—Sermons.
I. Title.
BT83.57.P66   261.8'09173'3   78-25970
ISBN 0-8170-0796-2

To Marion

*faithful partner in dialogue and ministry
with whom I have shared the joy and pain of
the liberation pilgrimage*

Contents

Preface

This book has emerged out of the confluence of two major streams of experience which I have had as a teacher of theology and as a pastor-preacher in a local congregation. The result is a work in applied theology which tries to ground a strategy for preaching in systematic theological analysis. Specifically, it is an attempt to use a hermeneutic of liberation to illuminate the task of the suburban preacher.

In recent years, I have had occasion to teach courses on the theology of liberation at the Candler School of Theology of Emory University and Andover Newton Theological School. That experience of testing the insights of a variety of liberation theologies in dialogue with students and colleagues confirmed in me a growing conviction of the need for a perspective in liberation theology which would address more directly the situation of middle-class suburban Americans.

My return, after eighteen years of college and seminary teaching, to the pastorate of a suburban congregation made this agenda an existentially urgent one for me. Moreover, it forced on me the necessity of grappling seriously with the dilemma of the suburban pastor caught in the tension of a concern for the liberation of the oppressed and a calling to minister to the liberation needs of one's own people. How does one proclaim the gospel out of that particular vocational tension? How does one remain faithful to both commitments without sacrificing either theological integrity or pastoral sensitivity? How does the ministry of preaching help to liberate captive suburbanites and, in turn, enlist them in a mission of reconciliation and liberation?

In what follows I make no claim to offer definitive answers to such questions. This book is not the report of a success story in suburban ministry. It represents, rather, the fruit of one person's struggle to forge a ministry out of the tensions which I believe faithfulness to the gospel in our kind of world imposes upon all of us. If the book helps some of my colleagues in ministry to work with those same tensions in more creative and liberating ways, it will have more than served its purpose.

I anticipate that some of my readers may feel uncomfortable with my profile of the suburban captive. They may allege that I am a prisoner of negative myths about the suburb which see it as a reactionary and privileged enclave, providing an escape from the problems and tensions of an urban society. John B. Orr and F. Patrick Nichelson have compiled data to challenge that stereotype in their book *The Radical Suburb*.[1] I am aware of the danger of pressing all suburbanites into a single, monolithic mold. I would warn the reader, therefore, that my characterization of the suburban ethos does not imply the claim that *all* suburbanites conform to a single type.

Another word of caution may also be in order. In using the term "suburbanite," I am not referring exclusively to the matter of geographical location but also to a particular kind of social grouping. Most suburbanites do live in the suburban fringes of the central cities of our nation. But there are many middle- and upper-middle-class people living in downtown apartment complexes or even in rural communities who, in attitudes and life-style, fit roughly into the description I have given of the suburban captive.

It would be ungracious of me not to acknowledge the contributions that others have made to the shaping of this project. I owe a theological debt to Jürgen Moltmann and Peter C. Hodgson who have helped me in the formulation of key perspectives on the problem of liberation. Initial drafts of some of the material were presented as papers to the Boston Theological Circle and the

---

[1] John B. Orr and F. Patrick Nichelson, *The Radical Suburb* (Philadelphia: The Westminster Press, 1970).

Ministers' Club of Boston, and I have profited from the critique of both of these groups. I am grateful to Dean George Peck and Professor Gabriel Fackre of Andover Newton Theological School for reading portions of the manuscript and giving me the benefit of their reaction and comments. I am also indebted to the congregation of the First Baptist Church of Lexington, Massachusetts, whose willingness to persevere with me in a pastor-people dialogue helped to provide the matrix out of which this project was born—and hopefully gained a measure of liberation for us both.

Good Friday,
1978

Alvin C. Porteous
Lexington, Massachusetts

Part One

Theological
Foundations

Chapter 1

Profile of the Suburban Captives

The last decade or so has witnessed the sudden emergence of a rash of liberation movements in our own country and around the world. Each new movement—whether it is of blacks, women, or oppressed people of the Third World—has opened up a fresh front in the struggle for freedom. Each movement has been an effort to break the shackles of a particular form of bondage and oppression. And each has developed its own version of a theology of liberation to articulate the meaning of its struggle and provide motivation and direction for its continued quest for more meaningful human freedoms.

Suburbia: A New Front for Human Liberation

One of the most critical fronts on which the battle for human liberation must be waged today lies in the predominantly white, affluent communities of suburban America. Here are the largest concentrations of wealth and power and political influence which can be used as instruments of either oppression or liberation. Here also is a freedom which is often more illusory than real, more external than internal, more economic and political than psychic and spiritual. For all their external freedom of movement, suburbanites are bound by the chains of inner fears, illusions, and guilts. Even people of goodwill are often unwittingly caught up in oppressive systems of institutional racism and sexism of which they are hardly even aware. Geographic separation, cultural insulation, and economic privilege make suburban dwellers particularly susceptible to false myths about how the other half lives, while the pervasive ideology of consumerism seduces them into embracing a shallow, inauthentic, materialistic life-style.

Recent liberation theologies have pointed to a two-fold source of human bondage and oppression. There is, first of all, the inner bondage of sin—the anxious, prideful, self-enslaving perversion of one's own freedom. In addition to this, however, there is the outer bondage of cultural, economic, and political oppression. Here we have sin writ large in society. Its enslaving effects are demonically reinforced by alienating institutions and structures as well as deceptive and oppressive ideologies and myths, which are the modern equivalents of the "principalities and powers" of Pauline theology.

This diagnosis of the situation of human bondage poses a double task for the achievement of human liberation. It calls not only for a psychic or spiritual liberation from sin but also a transformation of those "powers" in the economic and political spheres which are dehumanizing and oppressive. The Christian faith speaks to both dimensions of the human predicament. In a recent work on liberation theology, Peter Hodgson summarizes helpfully the perspective of the Christian gospel on the problem of human liberation:

> Christianity acknowledges the necessity of the struggle for political and economic liberation, and its gospel of the kingdom is a political gospel; but the freedom of which Christianity speaks has its ultimate source neither in politics nor in economics but in the word of God which liberates men and women by calling them forward into true communion with God and with each other—a realm of freedom in which each finds his or her own fulfillment in the fulfillment of the other.[1]

It is the thesis of this book that those of us who are called to preach to suburban captives must keep in constant tension these two foci (inner bondage of sin and outer bondage of oppression) of the mission of liberation, or else our efforts to proclaim a liberating gospel will be vitiated. A one-sided emphasis on personal, psychic liberation through the evangelical proclamation of grace not only runs the danger of "cheap grace," but it also fails to address the demonic objectifications of sin in socioeconomic, cultural, and

[1] Peter C. Hodgson, *New Birth of Freedom* (Philadelphia: Fortress Press, 1976), p. 111.

political institutions and structures. On the other hand, a simplistic call to social action and social change, no matter how prophetically it may be delivered, is bound to be ineffectual because it ignores the inner bondages on which oppressive ideologies and institutions feed and from which they derive their enslaving power. Only a holistic approach which sees the intrinsic connections between the bondage which comes from within and the oppression which comes from without can be genuinely liberating. If any real liberation is to occur, the evangelical indicative of personal salvation from the bondage of sin must be kept in dialectical tension with the prophetic imperative to transform social structures.

How does this analysis illuminate, in particular, our task of preaching to suburban captives? In this chapter I will attempt to sketch some of the dynamics of human bondage as they apply to the predominantly white, middle-class residents of suburbia who constitute the majority membership of our congregations. In the next chapter I will do the same for some of the dynamics of liberation contained in central affirmations of the Christian faith. In Part Two, I will develop the implications of these theological analyses for a strategy and style of preaching in the suburban church. Part Three will provide sermons which are examples of this style and strategy.

Many of the theologies of liberation of the last decade, particularly those written by some black theologians, have had little or no place in their fundamental categories for any project aimed at the liberation of white, middle-class suburbanites. They view their theology as a theology of and for "the community of the oppressed," from which suburbanites are rather obviously excluded. Operating from a hermeneutical perspective which involves a rigid dualism between the oppressor and the oppressed, such theologies can include white affluent Americans only under the category of the oppressor. One of the most extreme articulations of this view comes from the pen of James Cone:

> Black Theology cannot accept a view of God which does not represent him as being for blacks and thus against whites. Living in a world of white oppressors, black people have no time for a neutral God. . . . There is no use for a God who loves whites the *same* as blacks.[2]

Cone's unguarded statement, while understandable as an

---

[2] James H. Cone, *A Black Theology of Liberation* (Philadelphia: J. B. Lippincott Company, 1970), pp. 131-132.

expression of black rage against white oppression, fails to expose the root of the problem of human liberation, including black liberation. By projecting all evil on a particular oppressor group, and in effect demonizing it, he is unable to see the ways in which all oppression is the external fruit of an internal bondage which is no respecter of persons and groups.

This is not to deny the provisional theological legitimacy of the oppressor-oppressed distinction. According to biblical faith, God does judge the oppressor and acts to liberate the oppressed. Faithful prophetic discernment of how God is working in the world must take account of this distinction. This means, among other things, that privileged white suburbanites must find a way of accepting the judgment of blacks that they mirror the face of the oppressor. This is true if for no other reason than that they acquiesce in and profit from a system which oppresses minority people.

But this is not the end of the matter. The opposition between the oppressor and the oppressed remains permanently irreconcilable until we are prepared to recognize that *the oppressor is also a captive,* as much in need of liberation as those who are oppressed. What makes one an oppressor, in fact, is one's own captivity to self-enslaving forces which hold one's will in bondage. "To be a victim of oppression is one thing," writes Frederick Herzog, "to be possessed by evil, another. Sin makes of all men not the oppressed, but the possessed. . . ."[3]

This recognition of a universal human bondage not only relativizes the oppressor-oppressed duality but also affirms both the humanity and the redeemability of the oppressor. And no one has a greater stake in that than the oppressed themselves. If no good news of liberation can be preached to the oppressor, then the oppressed are of all men and women most miserable. For their yoke of oppression will continue to weigh heavily upon them until their oppressors are set free from the inner compulsions and drives which hold them captive.

One of the most difficult tasks facing the preacher is to break the suburbanites' illusion that they are already free and therefore in no need of liberation. One of the most cherished self-images of suburban dwellers is their sense of autonomy which they erroneously equate

[3] Frederick Herzog, *Liberation Theology* (New York: The Seabury Press, Inc., 1972), pp. 48-49. Copyright © 1972 by Frederick Herzog. Used by permission of The Seabury Press, Inc.

with freedom. The suburban way of life is built upon the assumption that one is guaranteed a "private space" in which one can work one's unfettered will in complete freedom without outside interference. A split-level home on a quiet street or a "summer place" at the lake is one's "castle" where one can do as one pleases. It occurs to such a person only with the greatest of difficulty that this very privacy, autonomy, and isolation may be forms of bondage which diminish one's humanity.

This illusion of freedom is reinforced in our culture by ideologies and slogans which suggest, as a matter of course, that "we live in a free country" and freedom is a commodity which we have inherited from our revolutionary ancestors. As one who preaches to a congregation in a suburban town which prides itself on being "the Birthplace of American Liberty," I can testify to how easy it is for people to confuse traditional freedoms with real freedom.

The problem is by no means new. Jesus met with the same resistance from people who thought themselves to be free and who resented the implications of being addressed as "captives." His liberating word to them was, as recorded in John 8:36, "If the Son makes you free, you will be free indeed."[4] The notion that they, of all people, needed to be liberated was offensive to them in the extreme. After all, they were reared in a long tradition of freedom, a tradition replete with many revered heroes and symbols of liberation. "We are descendants of Abraham, and have never been in bondage to anyone. What do you mean by saying, 'You will be made free'?" Frederick Herzog's commentary on this passage suggests how binding and blinding such a proud reliance on inherited freedom can be:

> We often think of freedom as our inherited and inalienable right. "We are Abraham's descendants". . . . No one dare say that "the children of the Reformation" are not free, or "George Washington's children." But true freedom has nothing to do with a mechanical handing on of privileges and rights from generation to generation. We are enslaved to external status symbols of traditional freedoms that actually keep increasing our concealment. Clinging to traditional freedoms often brings about new bondage. . . . Pride in inherited freedom is the opposite of true freedom.[5]

Goethe was undoubtedly right when he said, "No one is more of

---

[4] See Part Three for a Bicentennial sermon, "Free Indeed: Our Gospel of Liberation," on this text.

[5] Herzog, *op. cit.,* pp. 125-126.

a slave than he who thinks himself free without being so." That is why our efforts to proclaim release to suburban captives require as much clarity as possible about the nature of the bondage which enslaves them and at the same time makes them oppressors of others. In the remainder of this chapter, I shall attempt this clarification through a brief exposition of the way in which Paul's four categories of bondage—sin, death, law, and the powers—illuminate the contemporary realities of suburban captivity.[6]

Sin: The Basic Bondage

The basic bondage which underlies all other forms of "unfreedom" is sin. "Truly, truly, I say to you," said Jesus, "every one who commits sin is a slave to sin" (John 8:34). It is important to see that sin is a form of self-enslavement, a bondage which is self-inflicted. It is occasioned, though not caused, by the anxiety that stems from the human being's awareness that one is a mixture of finiteness and freedom, nature and spirit. The end result of one's desperate attempts to allay this anxiety is what Paul Ricoeur has referred to as "the paradox . . . of a man who is responsible *and* captive, or rather a man who is responsible for being captive—in short, the concept of the *servile will.*"[7]

There are two basic stratagems which people employ in a vain attempt to escape their anxiety over their identity as human beings. The one is idolatry, or pride. The other is apathy, or flight from responsibility. The one is the sin of presumed infinitude, setting oneself up as a god, deifying one's own freedom, power, and virtue. The other is the sin of a complacent and despairing finitude which seeks to escape from the risks and responsibilities of freedom by immersing oneself in the securities of the flesh.

Because of their relative power and wealth and their more expansive opportunities for self-expression, suburban captives may be more potently tempted by the sin of idolatry. They are easily tempted into regarding their own culture, values, and life-style as normative for all people. While they are relatively free from economic insecurity, their personal insecurity is such that they have to build themselves up at others' expense. In order to bolster their own fragile,

---

[6] Here I am indebted to Peter Hodgson's perceptive analysis in *op. cit.,* especially pp. 168-206.

[7] Paul Ricoeur, *The Symbolism of Evil,* trans. Emerson Buchanan (Boston: Beacon Press, 1967), p. 101.

threatened egos, they readily engage in a put-down of others—whether blacks or women or lazy welfare recipients. Archie Bunker has become the prototype of those so insecure in their own personhood that they have to people the earth with wops, gooks, kikes, and niggers. While Archie lives in Queens, his spirit is alive and well in the suburbs, though more subtle in expression.

Since the two basic forms of sin are dialectically related because of their common rootage in the experience of anxiety, the suburban captives are by no means immune to the sin of flight, or apathy, either. At least in part, the very phenomenon of suburban flight from the central cities can be regarded as a manifestation of this form of sin. The suburban mentality involves a deliberate attempt to put "out of sight and out of mind" the problems of the wider world beyond the safe and antiseptic haven of the suburbs. This calls for an anesthetizing of feeling and conscience so that it is no longer disturbed by the demands of responsible freedom in relation to human suffering and need beyond the suburban enclave.

Sin, in the form of apathy, is a disease of the spirit which is by no means limited to the suburbs, though its virulence is particularly strong there. "This apathy," writes Jürgen Moltmann, "is the sickness of our time, a sickness of person and systems, a sickness to death, to personal and universal death."[8] It gains strength in times of great societal stress like our own when the individual throws up psychic defenses to protect oneself against emotional overload. As the psychologist Rollo May describes it, "Apathy, or a-pathos, is a withdrawal of feeling; it may begin as playing it cool, a studied practice of being unconcerned and unaffected. . . . Apathy, operating like Freud's 'death instinct,' is a gradual letting go of involvement until one finds that life itself has gone by."[9]

A celebrated incident which occurred in 1964 in Kew Gardens in New York City startlingly dramatized the pathological nature of the apathy of our times. Thirty-eight respectable, law-abiding citizens looked on for more than half an hour as a killer stalked and stabbed a woman in three separate attacks. When questioned afterwards as to why they had not intervened in any way, they responded consistently, "I did not want to get involved."

[8] Jürgen Moltmann, *The Crucified God,* trans. R. A. Wilson and John Bowden (New York: Harper & Row, Publishers, 1974), p. 253.
[9] Rollo May, *Love and Will* (New York: W. W. Norton & Company, Inc., 1969), p. 30.

Apathy, it would seem, is the psychic mechanism that people use to guarantee their invulnerability by insulating themselves from the pains and problems of others. Recently a Sunday school teacher in a suburban church reported to me her perception of a heightened level of anxiety in her pupils when she began to illustrate biblical teachings with reference to problems of the inner city. Suburban preachers who give much time to the discussion of social issues with their congregations can give similar testimony. It is no accident that apathy goes hand in hand with the high premium that suburbanites place on the value of privacy. The apathetic suburbanite resists the intrusion of others into either one's geographical or emotional "space." Here is evidence enough that the true antithesis of love is not hatred but apathy and indifference.

But apathy which spurns the risks of responsible love and freedom inevitably leads to the captivity of boredom and inner emptiness. This, no doubt, is why so many have remarked about the sterility of the suburban life-style. This vacuity is not diminished but increased by the suburbanites' obsessive preoccupation with an ever-escalating materialistic standard of living. Their capitulation to the consumer mentality and their insatiable drive to acquire ever more consumer goods represent a vain attempt to ground their life's security and meaning within the bounds of a constricted finitude. It leads, in the terminology of Paul, to the bondage of life "according to the flesh" *(kata sarka)*. But this frantic grasping after life in terms of flesh and finitude is invariably self-defeating. The one who tries to save one's life in this way, according to Jesus, is bound to lose it. For true life is found only in openness to God, in the risk of responsible freedom, in the vulnerability of love.

The Enslaving Power of Death and Law

There are two other sources of bondage in Paul's list which reinforce the interior bondage of sin—death and law. Death, in the New Testament view, is the ultimate form of bondage whose deadly virus infuses and strengthens the grip of all the others. For the most part unacknowledged and repressed in our culture, it is, as Hodgson says, "the deadly power masked behind fear and anxiety, the guilty conscience, the repressions of civilization, and the aggression and destructiveness of the human species." [10]

---

[10] Hodgson, *op. cit.,* p. 191.

Death, as natural mortality, is not in itself a binding power. It becomes enslaving only when it is viewed apart from faith in God's sovereignty over it, only when it is invested with finality and ultimacy. Then it becomes the driving force behind the sinful flight from life and freedom. As Paul says, "The sting of death is sin" (1 Corinthians 15:56*a*). Death itself, in the sense of our mortal transiency and perishability, does not hold us captive. Rather, the sin of anxious unbelief in the face of death transforms death into a fearsome, oppressive power. Death then becomes the silent spectre which casts its shadow over the whole of life, the invisible virus which infects the bloodstream of the body politic as well as the life of the individual.

A nihilism which regards death as the final reality—as god— fuels the suburbanites' pursuit of a pseudo-life of materialistic and sensual satisfactions. Because they live, consciously or subconsciously, in fear of death as the ultimate horizon, suburbanites grasp greedily after the rewards and gratifications of their finite, worldly existence. Because of their anxiety over their own survival, they compete quite compulsively for a place in the sun which will give them the illusion of their own immortality.

One of the most significant findings of Freud's psychoanalytical research was that every person is unconsciously convinced of his or her own immortality. This helps to explain the widespread psychological denial of death in our culture. The way we cope with the anxiety over our own mortality is to deny it. Because of the massive cover-up of death in our society, some have referred to it as the new pornography. Death is a topic that is not talked about in polite conversation but gets dealt with, if at all, in the world of private fantasy.[11]

Such denial, however, does not draw the sting from death as a source of human bondage. The personal and social consequences of our avoidance of death are anything but liberating. Such devastating consequences on human freedom can be seen in the compulsive quests of modern men and women for immortality substitutes. Consider, for example, the "immortality trip" of the suburban executive who claws his way up the corporate ladder in order to occupy the "room at the top." Family, colleagues, competitors, the public interest—all may be sacrificed to his overweening desire to

[11] Cf. Richard W. Doss, *The Last Enemy* (New York: Harper & Row, Publishers, 1974), pp. 3, 9.

obliterate the reminders of his own finitude and make a mark which he hopes will survive the ravages of time. Or consider the suburban housewife and mother, hedged in by the social and cultural restraints of a male-dominated society, who feels she must secure her "immortality" through the lives and achievements of her children. Her hopes for lasting personal significance through her children are bound to be experienced by them as an oppressive weight.

There is a sobering paradox in our American attitude toward death which compounds its destructiveness. Denial of death goes hand in hand with a morbid obsession and fascination with it. Our cultural preoccupation with death, it would seem, is a subtle way of repressing it as an event of personal significance. One way of escaping the necessity of dealing with death as a personal, existential issue is to depersonalize it and routinize it, as is done night after night in the monotonous flow of mayhem and murder which assaults our sensibilities on prime-time television. If we can think of death impersonally in terms of images on a TV screen, statistics, or body counts, then we can keep it at arm's length and strip it of any real human meaning for ourselves. The ghastly result of this syndrome of escape is an ever-rising level of tolerance for violence, war, and oppression, and a growing insensitivity to their victims. Thus, the enslaving power of death, working through the mechanism of denial, can cause a whole society to orient itself toward death rather than life.

The law as a source of bondage is a familiar theme in Pauline theology. While in principle the law serves a worthy purpose as the revelation of God's will which provides a measure for right conduct and an instrument of justice in the world, the way the law works out in practice makes it a primary form of bondage. It becomes a symbol of human estrangement from true being—an alien, heteronomous power to be resisted in the name of freedom—and thus an inducement to sin further. On the other hand, it can become the opportunity for moralistic and legalistic self-justification which only binds men and women more tightly in the chains of idolatrous self-deception.

In a classical autobiographical description of human bondage in Romans 7, Paul talks about this profound ambiguity of law and the way it is linked in a vicious circle with sin and death: "Apart from the law sin lies dead. I was once alive apart from the law, but when the commandment came, sin revived and I died; the very commandment which promised life proved to be death to me. For sin, finding

opportunity in the commandment, deceived me and by it killed me"
(Romans 7:8b-11). It is as if law, which should have been on the side
of life and freedom, had conspired with sin to strengthen sin's
enslaving grip. When our goodness is grounded in legalism, when we
respond to the awakened consciousness of guilt by a self-justifying
observance of the law, the result is not freedom but a deeper bondage.
The spontaneity of freedom is replaced by a moralistic compulsive-
ness which tries desperately, but unsuccessfully, to establish its own
goodness. Thus, the law demonstrates its impotence to break the
captivity of "the servile will." And the last state of a person is worse
than the first. "Wretched man that I am!" Paul cries. "Who will
deliver me from this body of death?" (v. 24).

Jürgen Moltmann suggests a structural analogy between this
vicious circle of sin, law, and death, and systemic patterns of
oppression in the life of society which are linked together by a
network of negative feedbacks which makes them even more
intractable:

> There are clearly systems of a psychological, social and political nature
> which have become *fatal legalistic patterns.* They are vicious circles in
> which even the best leads to what is worse. They are therefore
> inescapable and without hope. They are processes of negative feedback
> in which orientation on life shifts over to become orientation on death.[12]

A good example of this is the complicated and frustrating
history of our nation's attempt to give meaningful substance to the
1954 Supreme Court decision on the desegregation of public
education. Clearly, that decision represented a landmark attempt to
redress a long-standing situation of discrimination and oppression.
But in its wake a scenario unfolded in which a complex maze of
psychological, cultural, legal, economic, and political forces fed into
one another in negatively reinforcing ways to frustrate the intent of
the decision and, in many cases, actually bring about counterproduc-
tive results.

Self-serving, foot-dragging politicians from the suburbs,
reflecting the racist attitudes of their constituents, used the legal
system to delay implementation as long as possible. Meanwhile
demagogic sloganeering which exploited cultural myths about
minorities produced an acceleration of white flight to the suburbs,
making rational planning for desegregation more difficult than

---

12 Moltmann, *op. cit.,* p. 293.

before. The compromises embodied in the desegregation plans because of resistance from whites frequently required greater sacrifices from blacks and poor whites than from more affluent suburbanites. Indeed, in many cases, suburbs sufficiently isolated from the inner-city ghettos were exempted completely. By the time implementation of court orders actually came about, the level of hostility was so high that interracial understanding and the breaking down of racial stereotypes—which were among the original goals of the desegregation effort—were impossible to achieve. Additionally, the general atmosphere of chaos generated by white resistance made real educational progress difficult for students of both minority and majority races. As a consequence, white suburbanites were confirmed in their original attitudes of superiority and self-righteousness and blacks in their despair and resentment.

In sum, a project with real potential for liberation of both blacks and whites was aborted, in many cases, by a vicious circle of psychological and systemic forces which conspired to tighten the chains of inner bondage to racial prejudice and the outer oppression of racial discrimination. Fortunately, not all attempts at racial desegregation present such a bleak picture. Where attempts have succeeded, it has been because a community has been able to summon up sufficient resources of moral goodwill to break the vicious circles which lead to death. Here is where the freedom of faith, expressing itself in liberating action in the social and political spheres can help to turn the tide.

As the above example illustrates, the way in which the notion of law functions in the culture of suburbia is highly interesting. By and large, suburbanites tend to be intensely moralistic and legalistic. They pride themselves on being law-abiding citizens while judging contemptuously the lawless elements of society which are ordinarily assumed to be among the black and the poor. (Crime in the executive suite is, of course, not considered as morally culpable as crime in the streets!) But this adulation of law and order, typical of the respectable suburbanites, paradoxically can be a way of sublimating and disguising their own awareness of guilt. "Racist societies," writes Peter Hodgson, "tend to be highly legalistic (e.g., the antebellum slave-holding states and present-day South Africa), because law provides a means both of social repression and of sublimating guilt feelings for the injustices perpetrated."[13]

[13] Hodgson, *op. cit.,* p. 190.

Our recent experience in the use of legislation to eliminate discrimination in education is a telling illustration of Hodgson's point. On the one hand, those who hold the preponderance of power are able to use the law to slow down progress toward desegregation and equality. On the other hand, when a minimal level of justice is secured by law, it may only serve to assuage their guilt and lead to a new entrenchment of the status quo, strengthened by the illusion that justice has now been achieved. Obedience to the law can thus provide a cover for continuing injustice and oppression while fostering the illusion of innocence.

Oppressive Ideologies and Social Structures

In our discussion of the enslaving power of the law, we have already anticipated the final link in the chain which forges our human bondage, according to the Pauline analysis. This final source of enslavement is summed up in Paul's doctrine of the "powers." These powers are of two kinds: heavenly or "spirit" powers—referred to variously as "angels," "principalities," "powers" (Romans 8:38), or "elemental spirits of the universe" (Galatians 4:3)—and earthly powers, or "the rulers of this age" (1 Corinthians 2:6).

These oppressive, demonic forces can be understood in a nonmythological way as the social objectification, in the external world of culture and politics, of the inner bondage of sinful idolatry. While these forces are a human creation, expressing prideful rebellion against God, they take on a power of their own which demonically reinforce tendencies toward idolatrous self-worship already present in the individual. Their power to oppress the minds and bodies of men and women cannot be neutralized by any strategy of liberation which is aimed exclusively at changing human hearts. As Hodgson explains in good Niebuhrian fashion,

> Not only are the pretensions and pride of a collective or social self more excessive than those of the individual ego, but also, by becoming a social and political phenomenon, bondage precedes the individual and ensnares him or her, despite one's own innocence and good intentions. Hence genuine liberation cannot be attained merely by a retreat into inwardness that leaves these objectifications untouched.[14]

When sin gets externalized in institutional structures, it must be dealt with in structural, i.e., sociopolitical, terms. That is why the demonic structures of institutional racism, for example, will not yield to moral

[14] *Ibid.,* p. 175.

suasion alone but will need to be brought under legal and political restraints.

The two categories of "powers" of which Paul speaks, the spiritual and earthly powers, need to be understood in their dialectical relationship with one another. To use the terminology of Marxism, the locus of the so-called "spirit" powers is to be found in the ideological superstructure of society, while the earthly powers refer to its economic and political infrastructure. It is perhaps not too big an interpretive leap to identify the Pauline principalities and powers with the ideologies which today serve to rationalize oppressive politico-economic structures and practices. Such ideologies are a compound of uncritical beliefs and emotion-laden images which distort our picture of social reality in ways which justify the privileged and the powerful in their domination and exploitation of others. These ideologies are binding and blinding illusions which cast a demonic spell over oppressors and oppressed alike, while legitimating and reinforcing the dehumanizing status quo.

Among the most obvious examples of enslaving and oppressive ideologies which afflict the suburban captive today are racism, sexism, and consumerism. Their demonic grip over the consciousness of people in the suburbs, as elsewhere, is strengthened by the fact that their influence over the human psyche is to a high degree unconscious rather than conscious. Participating in the self-deceiving nature of all sinful idolatry, these three ideologies cannot be dissolved merely by rational argument or enlightenment. Liberation from their power requires, as Hodgson puts it, "something like 'conversion' by means of . . . which the whole deceptive structure is brought into the harsh light of reality and dissipated." [15] As we shall see in the next chapter, preaching that is effective for liberation must be a form of consciousness-raising which breaks the spell cast over people by these false myths by which they live.

Religion and Ideological Enslavement

The role of religion in human liberation is as ambiguous as we have seen the role of law to be. While it can provide a liberating input into the vicious circles of bondage and oppression, it can also function to buttress ideological enslavement and forge more securely the chains of suburban captivity. Since I know it best, I would like to

[15] *Ibid.*, p. 197.

illustrate this point out of the history of my own Baptist denomination. Others can, I am sure, find similar evidence in their own denominational history and experience.

A bastardized understanding of the meaning of freedom in terms of individual autonomy, embraced by many Baptists, has helped to foster an exaggerated individualism which undercuts the corporate mission of the church in behalf of the oppressed. William R. McNutt, in a widely used manual of Baptist polity, typifies this extreme individualism. "The individual," he says, "is competent in all matters of religion." Soul competency "sets each man on a throne." It produces the rugged individual "tall, straight and clean as a Southern pine." [16] The very images he uses to talk about spiritual autonomy are masculine, triumphal images which suggest self-sufficiency, dominance, and control—images of the self-made man. Notice that there are no servanthood images—the surrendering of autonomy for the sake of others or the subjection in service to all God's children who suffer the pains of oppression.

Such religiously sanctioned individualism both reflects and reinforces the laissez-faire ideology so pervasive in American culture generally, an ideology which so readily becomes an instrument of oppression against the poor and the weak. Its ideological cast can be detected in the way it dissolves the basic paradox of Christian freedom as articulated, for example, in Luther's arresting formula: "A Christian is the most free lord of all, and subject to none; a Christian is the most dutiful servant of all, and subject to everyone"; Bonhoeffer, too, said that "freedom is not something man has for himself but something he has for others. . . . Being free means 'being free for the other. . . .'" [17]

Other examples could be cited of ideological overtones in Baptist beliefs, particularly in the forms in which they get popularized and politicized. Slogans about "soul liberty" and the separation of church and state (translated as separation of religion and politics) have exercised a pernicious influence in encouraging a withdrawal from the struggles for liberation in the economic and political spheres. Thus, Baptists, accompanied by Christians of other denominations, have had the ideological instruments at hand to

[16] William Roy McNutt, *Polity and Practice in Baptist Churches* (Valley Forge: Judson Press, 1959), pp. 21, 24, 32.

[17] Dietrich Bonhoeffer, *Creation and Fall* and *Temptation* (New York: Macmillan, Inc., 1959), p. 37.

enable them to slip easily into the bondages of suburban captivity.

The Suburban Captivity of the Churches

It is more than fifteen years since Gibson Winter wrote his prophetic, ground-breaking book *The Suburban Captivity of the Churches*. His thesis that the suburban church's abdication of responsibility for the metropolis contributes to the fracturing of the metropolitan community and the decay of the inner city is as true now as it was then. Indeed, the intervening years have seen the suburban noose drawn even more tightly around the dying central cities, with devastating consequences for their inhabitants. And the churches have continued to identify with the suburban community where their members live to the exclusion of the wider metropolitan community where they go for work and entertainment.

The other side of his thesis is equally relevant today, namely, that the introversion and exclusiveness of suburban churches rob them of their Christian identity. "The congregation," he wrote, "is first and foremost an economic peer group; it is secondarily a believing and worshiping fellowship." "For many people today, church member-ship means the opportunity to see the same people they meet at Kiwanis or the country club." The church's suburban captivity consists in "confusing social class and residential identity with the meaning of membership in the Christian community."[18]

Needless to say, this sociological homogeneity of the suburban church makes it highly vulnerable to the kind of ideological enslavement which we have just discussed. Such social uniformity also makes it easy for the church to slip into nonthreatening, socially approved roles which do not challenge, in any significant way, the stubborn realities of alienation and oppression.

Jürgen Moltmann has written that Christianity today "finds itself in a new Babylonian captivity"[19] because it has simply taken over for itself the role which society has assigned to it, namely, "the function of unburdening man."[20] By providing the inner assurances of personal religion, the warmth and responsiveness of a spontaneous fellowship, and a stable and predictably ordered institution, the

---

[18] Gibson Winter, *The Suburban Captivity of the Churches* (Garden City, N.Y.: Doubleday & Company, Inc., 1961), pp. 70-71, 172, 173.
[19] Jürgen Moltmann, *Religion, Revolution, and the Future*, trans. M. Douglas Meeks (New York: Charles Scribner's Sons, 1969), p. 117.
[20] *Ibid.*

church compensates for what is lacking in the alienating and depersonalizing life of the secular world. "With her circles and fellowships, she can fashion a Noah's Ark for the socially estranged and creates an island of cohumanity in the rough sea of a society which John Doe cannot change." [21]

If this is true of the church at large, it is preeminently true of the church in suburbia. Within limits, of course, this process of psychological unburdening can have a humanizing effect. Human beings need some relief from the depersonalizing pressures and debilitating uncertainties of modern society to preserve their humanity intact. But if this relief becomes the sole *raison d'etre* of the church, it loses its potential for liberation. When a church is content to be no more than a haven from society, discharging only socially sanctioned roles, it is already well on the way to captivity to the social status quo. It can no longer infuse the social order with any "ferment of freedom" by which its oppressiveness can be effectively challenged.

The profile of the suburban captive is not complete without the profile of a captive church—a church which has allowed its message to be distorted by enslaving ideologies and a church which has allowed its mission to be coopted to serve as a safety valve for an oppressive society. The church's captivity became even more pronounced in the seventies, as the backlash from the activism of the sixties resulted in a growing mood of resignation and extreme cultural accommodation. Even less than before is it prepared to "make waves" in the struggle for freedom. The suburban preacher committed to the task of human liberation occupies an exposed but strategic outpost in that ongoing struggle.

[21] *Ibid.*, p. 116.

Chapter 2

The Theological Dynamics of Liberation

The reminder at the close of the last chapter that religious ideas can serve, however unwittingly and indirectly, as instruments of ideological enslavement and oppression underlines the urgent need for a rethinking of widely held assumptions about the meaning of the Christian faith. Genuinely liberating preaching can flow only from a firm grasp of the theological dynamics inherent in biblical faith which press toward full human liberation. It will be our task in this chapter to try to identify some of the structural elements, motifs, and symbols in biblical faith which have liberating significance and power.

A Hermeneutic of Liberation

A sound hermeneutical approach is crucially important for such an undertaking. Hermeneutics involves a process of translation and interpretation which enables us to enter into the life and self-understanding of the biblical people of God in ways which have contemporary meaning and relevance. It is the way we go about making their story our story despite the historical and cultural gulf which separates us after two thousand years. Many persons are finding that the hermeneutical key which can unlock the strange world of the Bible and bring its message alive for us today is the theme of liberation, or, to be more precise, the theme of God's liberating word and action in Jesus Christ. They are discovering that the very character of the gospel as "Good News" derives from the fact that it consists of "variations on the theme" of liberation in Christ. In many periods of the church's history, the gospel has been simply handed down as a static tradition from the past without its explosive dynamic for liberation being either perceived or unpacked. Today that is changing. "Knowing that an unexamined history operates as a fate," Letty Russell writes, "liberation theologians are trying to seek out the meaning of Christian tradition so that it speaks the good news of liberation in concrete circumstances of oppression and liberates the minds and actions of people."[1] Their efforts are directed toward the "search for a usable past," the gospel in the tradition which is genuinely liberating rather than oppressive.

In all such attempts to rethink the central meanings of the Christian message in the context of the movement toward human liberation, two important findings have emerged. On the negative side, it has been discovered that many traditional theological formulations and images are actually dysfunctional as far as human liberation is concerned; in fact, they function as rationalizations of an oppressive, dehumanizing status quo, serving as ideologies of oppression rather than as an empowerment for liberation. On the positive side, the rediscovery and reemphasis of the theme of liberation is providing a fruitful interpretive instrument for opening up, in a fresh and credible way, authentic dimensions of the biblical message, long hidden from Christian eyes and repressed in the Christian consciousness.

In these ways, liberation theology is performing a therapeutic service, first of all to theology itself[2] and secondly to the Christian community. It has drawn attention, in a salutary and disturbing way, to the blind spots in our interpretation of Scripture that have resulted from our social and economic conditioning, and, more particularly, from the church's characteristically privileged status in society. Because the church has been so much the prisoner of middle-class cultural values, it has failed to see and appropriate the dynamic for liberation in the biblical sources of its faith. Jürgen Moltmann comments pungently on this ideological skewing of the church's message:

Reading the Bible with the eyes of the poor is a different thing from

[1] Letty M. Russell, *Human Liberation in a Feminist Perspective—A Theology* (Philadelphia: The Westminster Press, 1974), p. 85.
[2] Cf. Juan Luis Segundo, *The Liberation of Theology* (Maryknoll, N.Y.: Orbis Books, 1976).

reading it with the eyes of the man with a full belly. If it is read in the light of the experience and hopes of the oppressed, the Bible's revolutionary themes—promise, exodus, resurrection and Spirit—come alive. The way in which the history of Israel and the history of Christ blend with that of the hungry and oppressed is quite different from the way in which they have often been linked with the history of the mighty and rich.[3]

In what follows, I shall attempt to lay bare, in summary fashion, the essentials of the Christian message as a gospel of liberation. If any such attempt is to be authentic, it must be guided by a hermeneutical perspective which looks at the message of the Bible through the prism of the sufferings and hopes of the poor and the oppressed. This is by no means parochializing the gospel and restricting its applicability to oppressed minorities. As we have seen, there is a bondage which afflicts all men and women to which the gospel is relevant as a liberating power. But unless we take what Bonhoeffer called "the view from below," "the perspective of the outcast, the suspects, the maltreated, the powerless, the oppressed, the reviled,"[4] we shall miss the Bible's own point of view—and with it the only real possibility of liberation that is open to the privileged as well as the poor.

The Bible, after all, came out of a community of the oppressed, first the people of Israel and then the New Testament church. Its contents quite naturally reflect the experiences of an oppressed people, for whom the gospel was received as "good news to the captives," on their way toward liberation. Paul's reminder to the Corinthians that "not many of you were wise according to worldly standards, not many were powerful, not many were of noble birth" accurately reflects the sociological makeup of the early church. This sociological fact is not without its theological significance, the implications of which Paul goes on to elucidate. "God chose what is foolish in the world to shame the wise, God chose what is weak in the world to shame the strong, God chose what is low and despised in the world, even things that are not, to bring to nothing things that are" (1 Corinthians 1:27-28).

This is the real "scandal of particularity" in the gospel—not simply that God has revealed himself at a particular point in history through a specially chosen people, but that those whom God has

[3] Jürgen Moltmann, *The Church in the Power of the Spirit,* trans. Margaret Kohl (New York: Harper & Row, Publishers, 1977), p. 17.
[4] Dietrich Bonhoeffer, *Letters and Papers from Prison,* The Enlarged Edition (New York: Macmillan, Inc., 1972), p. 17.

chosen to receive and disseminate his revelation are not drawn from the ranks of the rich and the powerful but the poor and the oppressed. The old Israel had its beginnings with a band of runaway slaves who before their liberation had provided cheap labor for the Egyptian pharaohs. The new Israel, the church, was chiefly drawn from the "marginals" of society, the wretched of the earth, the moral failures, the politically powerless, and the religiously ostracized.

Since the life situation *(sitz im leben)* out of which biblical faith was born was characterized by massive social and political as well as religious oppression, it is not surprising that that faith should take the form of a message of liberation. It is not surprising either that in postbiblical times, as Christianity entered into alliances with the wealthy and the powerful and finally became the established religion of society, the liberating dynamics of primitive Christian faith were more and more suppressed. In view of this development, there may be a good deal of truth in the charge that the Christian people of the Western World have been "'badly christened' in so far as they accept and obey the liberating gospel only in a highly sublimated form— which leaves the reality unfree as it was before."[5] Certainly the orthodox interpretations of the faith which have dominated the history of Western Christianity have provided little leverage for liberating change in society and in many cases have actually served as ideological supports for a system of oppression.

Today we are faced with the difficult task of disentangling the message of the gospel from these ideological accretions and distortions and allowing its latent dynamics for liberation to be released. For this to happen, the Christian consciousness must get in fresh touch with the story of freedom and emancipation in the Bible. It must find ways of appropriating both the understanding and the practice of freedom which energized the biblical people of God in the new settings of bondage and oppression which exist today.

This task, as J. B. Metz has rightly observed, entails the activation of a "dangerous and liberating memory."[6] The exercise of memory, of course, does not always have to involve us in consequences that are either liberating or dangerous. When memory takes the form of nostalgia, it simply facilitates a flight into the past to

[5] Herbert Marcuse, *Eros and Civilization: A Philosophical Inquiry into Freud* (Boston: Beacon Press, 1966), p. 70.

[6] Cited in Hans Küng, *On Being a Christian,* trans. Edward Quinn (Garden City, N.Y.: Doubleday & Company, Inc., 1976), p. 121.

avoid the present pain of liberation. Some biblicist forms of preaching practice this as a fine art, with the result that the chains of our present bondage are drawn all the more tightly.

It is a different matter, however, when preaching activates our memory of the biblical past as the history of God's liberating mission on behalf of the oppressed. Such an aroused memory can be a subversive force to disrupt the status quo of the present by undermining the notion that the unfreedom that we experience in the present is either inevitable or normative. The memory of God's promises of freedom enacted through Jesus Christ is a subversive memory which stands in tension with every enslaving reality.

The situation that confronts virtually every suburban preacher today is one of widespread amnesia—a massive forgetfulness of our Christian roots in the biblical community of faith. The television program "Roots" has forcefully reminded us of the crisis of identity which occurs when a people are cut off from their historical roots and lose all memory of the communal history which defines who and what they are. Amnesia, individual or corporate, means a tragic loss of identity. Theodore O. Wedel has speculated about what would happen to our national life if Americans corporately were to suffer amnesia. We would lose our identity as a people and all clues as to what being an American means. "Yet an analogous fate," he writes, "threatens . . . the illiterate Christianity of suburbia unless it recovers its identity by way of memory of its historical past."[7]

It would be simplistic to assume, however, that the problem of Christian identity today is merely one of factual illiteracy about biblical history. What is needed is not simply a recovery of biblical facts but of their experiential meaning and relevance for human liberation as well. Somehow the biblical story of God's liberating action in history must become our story if an authentic Christian identity is to be formed in the individual and in the church. Any real activation of Christian memory requires that we ourselves step out of the audience and become actors in God's still unfinished drama.

Jürgen Moltmann begins one of his sermons with the arresting statement: "The impression that a Christian man is a free man who disseminates liberation is seldom publicly generated."[8] That is a

[7] Theodore O. Wedel, *The Gospel in a Strange, New World* (Philadelphia: The Westminster Press, 1963), p. 16.

[8] Jürgen Moltmann, *The Gospel of Liberation,* trans. H. Wayne Pipkin (Waco, Tex.: Word Books, 1973), p. 53.

measure of the toll that the modern Christian identity crisis has taken. The preacher can contribute to the reversal of that sad state of affairs not simply by the recital of biblical facts but, as we shall see in the next chapter, through engaging in a form of consciousness raising which creates fresh resonances for the biblical message of liberation. Such a style of preaching, however, requires a clear perception of the theological dynamics of liberation imbedded in that message. And to a discussion of these dynamics we now turn.

God as the Power of Liberation

The history of Christianity, at least from the Constantinian era to the present (with some notable exceptions) provides less than reassuring evidence that belief in God functions as a significant dynamic in human liberation. In fact, the case has often been made that repressive images and ideas of God generated in the church have produced the fertile soil out of which modern atheism has sprung. Ironically, God has come to be seen by many as the enemy of freedom rather than its ally and sponsor. When God is represented as the supreme Guardian of law and order and the ultimate sanction for a status quo which is oppressive and dehumanizing, then there is no alternative for those who hunger for freedom than to revolt against such a God. Carl Braaten describes the logic of this development as follows:

> We can understand atheism as a revolution of freedom against the idea of God as the ultimate source of authoritarian relations in society. The slavish mentality among Christians that so nauseated Nietzche can be traced to the picture of God as absolute legislator. Belief in God as the last sanction of the established world order was diagnosed as the root cause of slavish social relations. To accelerate the struggle for freedom, it was necessary to proclaim the "death of God."[9]

The tragedy of this modern denial of God in the name of human freedom lies in the fact that an accurate perception of the God of biblical faith would have rendered such a denial unnecessary. In essence, what modern atheism is revolting against is not the God of the Bible but an ideological distortion which is the product of human idolatry. The Bible, in both Old and New Testaments, witnesses consistently to a God who, far from stifling the impulse of freedom, is the transcendent power of liberation by which freedom is actualized

[9]Carl E. Braaten, *Christ and Counter-Christ* (Philadelphia: Fortress Press, 1972), p. 35.

in history. José Míguez Bonino has helpfully described how the biblical God acts in history as a dynamic of liberating change:

> For the Bible, God is not the eternally Present One who renders superfluous the movement of history or the eternal Reason who enables man to understand—and therefore to accept—things as they are, but the freedom which intervenes in history in order to prevent the past from determining the future. He is the freedom that impregnates history for the birth of a discontinuous possibility; he is the subverter of the status quo.[10]

There are two paradigmatic events in Scripture through which God identifies himself definitively as the Liberator of oppressed humanity; the Exodus and the resurrection. The one dominates the Old Testament and the other the New. These two pivotal events in the divine mission of liberation to which the Bible bears witness constitute critical reference points for understanding God's distinctive self-identification as Liberator.

In a preface to the Commandments of the covenant, God's identity is linked with the decisive act of liberation by which a nondescript band of Hebrew slaves became a free people. "I am the LORD your God, who brought you out of the land of Egypt, out of the house of bondage" (Exodus 20:2). This theme of God's liberating intervention in the history of Israel, which is the basis of its own identity as God's covenant people, reappears like a refrain in many of the Old Testament writings. God had broken open a future for them which had been closed in both objective and subjective ways: objectively because of the oppressive power of their Egyptian taskmasters and subjectively because of their own "slave mentality" which prevented them from summoning up on their own the motivation and energy to throw off their yoke of oppression.[11] The symbolism of the Exodus suggests that God can be experienced as the power of liberation in a two-fold way, loosening the grip of oppressive social and political structures, while also providing an inner psychic emancipation from the fears and self-doubts which make us willing slaves.

The counterpart in the New Testament to the liberating event of the Exodus is the resurrection. Just as God was named and identified in the Old Testament as the one "who brought you out of the land of

---

[10] José Míguez Bonino, *Doing Theology in a Revolutionary Situation* (Philadelphia: Fortress Press, 1975), p. 76.

[11] Cf. *ibid.,* p. 77.

Egypt, out of the house of bondage," so in the New Testament he is identified by name as the one "who raised Christ Jesus from the dead" (see Romans 8:11), the God "who gives life to the dead and calls into existence the things that do not exist" (4:17*b*). In both cases, as Jürgen Moltmann points out, God gets his proper name from an historical act of liberation which brings freedom to those involved: "in the one case it brings the people freedom from a historical tyrant, in the other it brings Jesus freedom from the tyranny of death." [12]

The resurrection differs from the Exodus in that, for New Testament faith, it is seen as an eschatological event which has liberating implications not only for the whole of humanity but for the cosmos as well. The resurrection brings freedom from the tyranny of death not simply to Jesus, but it also gains it for the entire created universe. As a consequence of the resurrection, Paul affirms, "the creation itself will be set free from its bondage to decay and obtain the glorious liberty of the children of God" (8:21).

We will miss the full range of available dynamics of liberation in the resurrection faith if, as is often done, we think of it exclusively as a guarantee of personal survival after death. "The last enemy to be destroyed" (1 Corinthians 15:26) is not simply physical death but everything which is deadly in life. Every system where "the powers of death" hold sway, where life and liberty are suppressed, is marked for extinction by virtue of "the power of the resurrection."

In this light, the resurrection must be seen as an act of the recreating power of God which opens up a new future of freedom for the world. The cross and resurrection represent history's most radical reversal. Whereas before, the powers of death, oppression, and alienation seemed to control the future, now their future has been taken away. The future henceforth belongs to freedom and the "new humanity" pioneered by Jesus. It belongs to "shalom," the kingdom of peace and justice which he announced as being at hand.

The resurrection creates a horizon of eschatological hope which is essential to mobilize and sustain any liberation struggle. The history of our recent past, in the wake of Vietnam and Watergate, has done much to generate an immobilizing mood of cynicism and pessimism about the possibilities of liberation. It has become easy to believe that the future lies with the selfish and corrupt manipulators of power or with the impersonal and brutal forces of history which

[12] Jürgen Moltmann, *The Crucified God,* trans. R. A. Wilson and John Bowden (New York: Harper & Row, Publishers, 1974), p. 189.

ride roughshod over human values and personal freedoms and make a mockery of justice. But the Easter faith authorizes us and empowers us to believe that, appearances notwithstanding, the future is still open. It makes sense to keep on hoping and working for a more human future. For the decisive breakthrough in the struggle for human liberation has already been achieved in the resurrection of our Lord. And now, as Paul said, "he must reign until he has put all his enemies under his feet" (15:25).

Such resurrection talk, however, can sound unrealistically triumphal, if not Pollyanish, in a world where the enemies of Christ and of human freedom are still very much on the loose. Resurrection talk can be credible in our kind of world, and hence serve as an effective dynamic for liberation, only if it stays in touch with the realism of the cross.

The cross of Christ occupies center stage in the drama of God's liberating action in history. It stands as a reminder that genuine liberation comes only through suffering—by God as well as by human beings. God's mission of liberation in the world is no simple success story—it suffers setbacks and defeats along the way. God's power to liberate, as Hodgson reminds us, is not exercised painlessly and effortlessly through "mighty, visible, miraculous incursions into history, after the fashion of a *Deus ex machina,* which a literalistic reading of the Exodus and resurrection stories alone—apart from the defeats suffered by God's people throughout history—might lead one to suppose." [13] Rather, God gives his freeing power in the form of a "suffering, liberating love" which endures the agony and rejection of his Son on the cross as his own pain.

In his book *The Crucified God,* Moltmann gives powerful expression to this understanding of a suffering God. While his exposition is too complex to summarize briefly, an incident which he quotes from *Night,* a book written by Elie Wiesel, a survivor of Auschwitz, captures in a moving way the central point of his theology of the cross:

> The SS hanged two Jewish men and a youth in front of the whole camp. The men died quickly, but the death throes of the youth lasted for half an hour. "Where is God? Where is he?" someone asked behind me. As the youth still hung in torment in the noose after a long time, I heard the man call again, "Where is God now?" And I heard a voice in myself answer:

[13] Peter C. Hodgson, *New Birth of Freedom* (Philadelphia: Fortress Press, 1976), p. 293.

"Where is he? He is here. He is hanging there on the gallows. . . ."[14]

Only a God who hangs on the gallows, a crucified God, a God who feels the pain of the world's oppressions in his own being, can be an effective power for liberation in a world where things like Auschwitz can still happen. Of course, the last word in faith's reading of human history is not God on the gallows or hanging on the cross. That would mean the end of the history of liberation and the death of God. The resurrection holds out the promise that the God "who gives life to the dead and calls into existence the things that do not exist" is capable of turning the darkest defeat into the most glorious victory, the most intractable oppressions into new possibilities of freedom. In the cross, God experienced along with Jesus all the characteristic forms of human bondage which we analyzed in the last chapter—sin, death, law, and the worldly powers—taking them into his own being and thus neutralizing their deadly oppressive power. In the godforsakenness of Jesus' abandonment on the cross it may have seemed as if the swaggering principalities and powers of the world had won the day. But that was only superficially the case. As Paul puts it so vividly, in this event of suffering love God was really nailing the bonds of oppression to the cross. "He disarmed the principalities and powers and made a public example of them, triumphing over them in him" (Colossians 2:15).

The secret of the resourcefulness of God's suffering love in overcoming oppression, as Moltmann and others have pointed out, is his trinitarian nature.[15] The Trinity has nothing to do with a closed circle of static relationships within the Godhead. It is a description of the history of God's liberating dealings with the world, in which he goes out from himself in suffering identification with his oppressed creation in order to gather it up into his own life of freedom and joy. The implications of this dynamic view of the Trinity are eloquently expressed in this statement from Moltmann:

> God experiences history in order to effect history. He goes out of himself in order to gather into himself. He is vulnerable, takes suffering and death on himself in order to heal, to liberate and to confer new life. The history of God's suffering in the passion of the Son and the sighings of the Spirit serves the history of God's joy in the Spirit and his

---

[14]Cited in Moltmann, *The Crucified God,* pp. 273-274.
[15]Cf. Moltmann, *The Crucified God,* pp. 235ff., and *The Church in the Power of the Spirit,* pp. 50-64.

completed felicity at the end. That is the ultimate goal of God's history of suffering in the world.[16]

It should be noted that the scandal in such an interpretation of the Trinity is no longer the speculative one of trying to conceive of how God can be three persons in one. It is the more existential scandal of a God who gets too close to us and threatens our independence and privacy. It is also the scandal of a vulnerable, suffering love which judges the apathy and indifference by which we try to shore up our own invulnerability. If, as we have seen in the first chapter of this book, privatism and apathy are twin distinguishing marks of suburban captivity, then the dynamics for liberation in the preaching of the triune God should be obvious.

Conversely, it should not be surprising that suburbanites, in particular, should resist such an image of God and replace it with an idol of their imagination which reflects more adequately their private, apathetic life-style and with which they can live more comfortably. The specifications for such a god call for one who is sufficiently remote that he does not encroach on their private turf. The suburbanites call for an *apathetic god* who is incapable of feeling and suffering with others or of opening them up to do the same. As Juan Luis Segundo has said, "Christians evince a persistent tendency to reject in practice the notion of an incarnate God; and to reduce it to the notion of an inaccessible God who is perfectly happy *in se*."[17] Such a tendency is particularly strong in suburbia. The image of God and our relationship to him with which suburbanites feel most comfortable are devastatingly described by Segundo: "God and we are like retired old men, shut off within the boundaries of our private estates, kept apart by their fences and by their own conception of what is due them."[18]

The power to liberate from such apathy and isolation is the power of the triune God, who draws us into his own history of suffering love and frees us for vulnerability and involvement in the liberation of others.

Jesus as the Agent of Liberation

In order for God to be an effective power of liberation in the world, he needs an historical agent or representative who actually

---

[16] Moltmann, *The Church in the Power of the Spirit*, p. 64.
[17] Juan Luis Segundo, *Our Idea of God* (Maryknoll, N.Y.: Orbis Books, 1974), p. 68.
[18] *Ibid.*

enters into history to enter into contest with the structures of bondage and oppression and unleash the dynamics of liberation. Without such a "stand-in," God remains in transcendent aloofness with no effective leverage on the vicious circles which hold history captive to its oppressive past. According to Christian faith, Jesus is God's "stand-in," his chosen agent to break the chains of that captivity and open history up to a liberating future. He is the instrumentality through which God's transcendent will to freedom becomes immanent in history, acquiring both concrete definition and liberating efficacy.

Ernst Käsemann has written that "freedom can never be carried to excess; it can always be inadequately represented."[19] Freedom is a "weasel word" with very fluid connotations and notoriously subject to ideological distortion and exploitation. It can serve as the watchword for ideologues of the right or the left. Repressive reactionaries and fanatical revolutionaries both justify their actions in the name of freedom. Freedom can be confused with autonomy and independence just as license and libertinism can be mistaken for liberty. Without a concrete criterion for judging freedom, its invocation by the partisans of freedom can lead to anything but true liberation.

Hence the urgent need for an adequate representation, a concrete definition of freedom! Christians find such a representation, such a definition, in the person and ministry of Jesus, the incarnate manifestation of God's will and action to liberate the oppressed. As the title of Käsemann's book so aptly expresses it, *Jesus Means Freedom*.

Jesus represents, for Christian faith, *the presence of liberated life* in the midst of the old dying orders of bondage and alienation. As "the first-born among many brethren" (Romans 8:29), he was chosen of God to pioneer a "new humanity," "a new way of being human."[20] The presence of liberated life in the person and mission of Jesus provides us with the model of an authentic human existence destined to supersede the old inauthentic mode of existence produced by thralldom to sin, law, death, and the powers.

This is the gist of Paul's doctrine of the "second Adam." Christ, as the "second Adam," is the decisive breakthrough in God's history

---

[19] Ernst Käsemann, *Jesus Means Freedom* (Philadelphia: Fortress Press, 1970), p. 59.

[20] Cf. my analysis of Christian existence as a new way of being human in *The Search for Christian Credibility* (Nashville: Abingdon Press, 1971), chapter 6.

of liberation. "What mankind could not do, this man did. In Adam all died, but in this second Adam is new life to be found. Here is the first of a new race. He loosened the grip of the powers on the future. He pushed open its door. Now we can go through!"[21]

As the pioneer of a liberated humanity, Jesus is the preeminently free person. A Christology of liberation must describe the dynamics of Jesus' own freedom as it serves as a paradigm for human liberation. There are three identifying marks of Jesus' freedom which provide criteria for distinguishing true freedom from its many counterfeits. As a radically free person, Jesus lived in complete openness to God, in total availability to others, and out of a fully integrated selfhood.[22] In him, the fundamental alienations of a fallen humanity were wholly overcome. That is why Tillich is able to see in him the perfect historical expression, under the conditions of estranged existence, of "the New Being." "According to the biblical picture of Jesus as the Christ, there are, in spite of all tensions, no traces of estrangement between him and God and consequently between him and himself and between him and his world (in its essential nature)."[23]

The deepest secret of Jesus' freedom was his complete openness and total abandonment to the one whom he characteristically referred to as "Father." There was a perfect identity between his own finite, human will and the will of the Father, whose servant-representative he conceived himself to be. "My food is to do the will of him who sent me, and to accomplish his work" (John 4:34).

This identification with the Father's will is misunderstood as a stoic submission to necessity, a knuckling under to a superior force. Jesus' servanthood and sonship were completely uncoerced. Jesus' obedience was freely given. Here was no automaton playing out a script decreed in advance. "Although he was a Son, he learned obedience through what he suffered" (Hebrews 5:8). His perfect unity with God was no automatic thing. That unity, and the radical freedom which flowed from it, was won by dint of human struggle and temptation.

The wilderness temptations at the beginning of his public

[21] Gabriel Fackre, *The Rainbow Sign: Christian Futurity* (Grand Rapids, Mich.: Wm. B. Eerdmans Publishing Company, 1969), p. 54.

[22] For a more technical analysis of these structures of freedom in Jesus, cf. Hodgson, *op. cit.,* chapter 5.

[23] Paul Tillich, *Systematic Theology,* Three volumes in one (Chicago: University of Chicago Press, 1975), Volume 2, p. 126.

ministry clearly depict an agonizing struggle with demonic options for discharging his mission of liberation, options which would have perverted the true meaning of freedom. The agony of Gethsemane at the end of his ministry represents his struggle, under the looming shadow of the cross, to maintain his faithfulness to his God-appointed mission at a time when it became evident that liberation could be won only through the dark night of suffering, through "obedience unto death" (see Philippians 2:8). His prayer "nevertheless not my will, but thine, be done" (Luke 22:42b) expresses his climactic acceptance of the logic of his mission of liberation as one of suffering servanthood. His cry "My God, my God, why hast thou forsaken me?" (see Mark 15:34) from the cross is a stubborn affirmation of filial obedience even in the face of deepest doubt, as the seemingly victorious forces of sin and death engulf his spirit.

While we must be careful to avoid the errors of a docetism which reduces Jesus to a nonhuman apparition in whom the dynamics of liberation do not really come into play, we must be equally sensitive to the dangers of the opposite heresy of ebionitism which leaves Jesus' freedom finally unexplained. The ebionite picture of Jesus as simply an extraordinary human being who won his freedom through heroic struggle suggests falsely that, in the final analysis, the new humanity in Jesus was a creation of his own will and decision. His faith and freedom, according to this view, were basically a human achievement rather than a gift of divine grace.

But precisely because Jesus maintained a consistent posture of life under grace, he was the radically free person and able to be the very incarnation of liberated life. Because his life was so dominated and empowered by grace, he could run the risks of freedom from which ordinary human beings characteristically retreat. That is why he was free to defy respectable conventions (eating with tax collectors and sinners), to shatter cultural stereotypes (relating to women freely on a basis of equality and respect), to relativize the laws of religion and piety (proclaiming that "the sabbath was made for man, not man for the sabbath"), and to spurn ordinary securities ("the Son of Man has nowhere to lay his head"). Empowered by grace, he also had the freedom to risk conflict with the principalities and powers of his time in both their religious and political forms and the freedom to sustain his challenge to their oppressive power even to the point of death.

In these and other expressions of his freedom, Jesus stands forth as the free person *par excellence* and as the contagious disseminator of freedom to others. But the power of Jesus' freedom was not self-derived. Its inner dynamic came from the liberating power of God uniquely at work in him to make him the representative and agent of divine liberation. His unconditional openness and obedience to God, whose Servant and Son he was, were the real source of his freedom.

Ernst Käsemann has observed that it is the First Commandment ("you shall have no other gods before me") which constitutes "the basis of human freedom and the sum of all theology and real piety."[24] When men and women honor that Commandment by directing their faith and loyalty exclusively to God, their world is cleared of all finite gods that would hold them in idolatrous captivity. The bondage to idols of race and sex and wealth and power is broken. So it was with Jesus to an absolute degree, as he lived his life in perfect unity with God through the exercise of an obedient and faithful sonship. Thus he was able to model for us the freedom of faith which alone is able to deliver us from captivity to the pseudo-gods of this world.

Freedom, not only in the form of faith but also in the form of love, is concretely represented for us in Jesus. Jesus' freedom was marked not only by a complete openness to God but by *a total availability to others.* Jesus was not only free *from* the inner bondages which forge the chains of human captivity, but he was also free *for* others, free to love the neighbor and minister to the poor, free to exercise public responsibility for the liberation of the captives. His very identity was defined by his ministry to others. His very being was a "being with and for others" (Bonhoeffer). His humanity mirrored the new humanity in the form of cohumanity. He was, above all else, "the gracious neighbor," the humble servant who gave himself radically to others in a ministry of self-emptying love. "The Son of Man came not to be served but to serve" (Matthew 20:28a).

In suburbia, such a picture of Christ is bound to be seen as scandalous. It challenges all the typical suburbanite's cherished images of freedom and selfhood. For him or her, the good life is defined predominantly in terms of the values of privacy. To be free is to be immunized against nagging reminders of the world's suffering. It is to be able to pull down one's window shades and draw into one's private world. Freedom means retreat into the private self and abdication of public responsibility. It is to be able to order one's private life as much as possible without external constraints of any kind. Freedom, so conceived, is synonymous with private autonomy.

[24] Käsemann, *op. cit.,* p. 32.

Such images of freedom translate into nonavailability to others, into withdrawal and separation, particularly from those who differ from us economically, culturally, and racially. It was Sartre who said that "hell is other people." For those of us with the suburban mentality, hell is other people who, because they are unlike us, threaten the insulated homogeneity of our residential ghetto. Hell is other people who, because they are victims of society's injustice, lay an uncomfortable claim on our compassion and our sense of corporate responsibility.

Jesus reveals our true humanity as a corporate rather than a private self and our true freedom as freedom for others rather than a freedom for self-enhancement. Such a disclosure shows up the preoccupation with the private self which is so common in suburbia as a form of slavery. "To worship one's beautiful private self is enslavement. To be related to corporate selfhood through Jesus is freedom."[25]

Since the Jesus of the Gospels brings under judgment the idolatry of the private self, it is not surprising that in the popular piety of suburbia he has had to undergo considerable metamorphosis. He has been spiritualized and sentimentalized beyond all recognition. He has become a purely personal Savior who warms the heart but does nothing to stoke the fires of compassion for the wretched of the earth or enlist men and women in the corporate work of liberating love.

But this co-opting of Jesus to reinforce the private and privileged life-style of suburbia can find no justification on biblical grounds. The parable of the last judgment in Matthew 25:31-36 makes this abundantly clear. Here the identification of Jesus with the hungry, the thirsty, the strangers, the naked, the sick, and the imprisoned is complete. The way we respond to them, in self-giving love or in apathetic indifference, is the way we respond to him. "As you did it to one of the least of these my brethren, you did it to me."

Here it is not simply a matter of ethics—the question of our moral obligation to the poor—which is at issue. At a deeper level, it is our own salvation and liberation which are at stake. The parable depicts an eschatological judgment which occurs at the end of history. It is the Christ hidden in the poor and destitute who will determine our final destiny. But that judgment is already working itself out in the here and now. Those who wall themselves off from the

[25] Frederick Herzog, *Liberation Theology* (New York: The Seabury Press, Inc.), p. 64.

world's suffering and needy are already in the process of giving up their humanity. Those who give themselves in selfless service to the hungry, the destitute, and the oppressed are already on the way to being liberated. In their brotherhood with the least of Christ's brethren, they are discovering what it means to be truly human. This is the significance of Jesus' saying "Whoever would save his life will lose it; and whoever loses his life for my sake and the gospel's will save it" (Mark 8:35).

Jesus' freedom, as we have seen, was characterized by both sonship and servanthood—a radical openness to God and an unconditional availability to others. A third mark of his freedom can be described as *the inner integrity and authority which flow from a fully liberated life.*

This mark was not something to which Jesus himself drew attention; it simply impressed itself on everyone who came into his presence and listened to his words. They experienced him as one who, to use the parlance of today's youth, "had his thing together." No inner conflicts rooted in anxiety or guilt incapacitated him for his mission. No alienation from his body produced any traces of asceticism or repression. He was able to celebrate life in its fullness with playfulness and joyous abandon. "The Son of Man has come eating and drinking; and you say, 'Behold a glutton and drunkard'" (Luke 7:34). His life and his teaching, his actions and his words, were perfectly consistent with one another; so there was no need for subterfuge or concealment. Neither was there any need to justify himself or his words with reference to external tradition and authority. His contemporaries "were astonished at his teaching, for he taught them as one who had authority, and not as their scribes" (Matthew 7:28-29). His person and his words had a self-authenticating quality, a transparency about them which convinced those who saw and heard him that in him they were in touch with the authoritative, liberating presence of God himself. And, at the same time, they saw in the integrity of his personhood what it means to be truly free and fully human.

Salvation as the Experience of Liberation

We have seen how Jesus serves as God's agent of liberation by incarnating the very essence of authentic freedom and liberated life. But this is not itself enough to set us free. It is not sufficient to be confronted with a model of true freedom for the dynamics of liberation to become effective in our own experience. In fact, the example of a truly free person can be intimidating to those who are still in bondage. It can be seen as an ideal so far beyond their reach that they are left in despairing resignation. Or it can register as a judgment on their unfreedom which they resist with defensive rationalizations and sometimes, as in the case of Jesus' enemies, with hostility and violence. In either case, the chains of their bondage are only reinforced.

"For freedom Christ has set us free," wrote Paul to the Galatians (5:1*a*). To understand fully the dynamics of that liberation, we must move beyond the perspective of the historical Jesus and the example of freedom which he set to a doctrine of salvation which elucidates the way in which his freedom gets actualized in our experience. The story of Jesus' freedom must be told in such a way that it becomes no longer a law which judges but, rather, a gospel which liberates.

There is no doubt that, for New Testament faith, it is the cross that represents the transition from the one to the other. Not only is the cross—the unsurprising result of his challenge of the established religious and political orders—the climax of Jesus' own history of freedom, but the cross is also the climactic event in the history of God's liberating activity, whereby men and women are reconciled to him and the powers of their bondage are decisively broken. It is the cross which forms the bridge between Jesus' freedom and "the glorious liberty of the children of God" (Romans 8:21*b*). It is the Christ who is crucified and now risen who is "the power of God for salvation to every one who has faith . . ." (1:16*b*).

It is the task of a doctrine of salvation to describe the dynamics by which the freedom of Christ is mediated to us as a present experience. Unfortunately, many traditional understandings of salvation have narrowed the scope of salvation so drastically that the full range of its liberating implications for life have been missed. It has been reduced to a purely individualistic and otherworldly transaction between the soul and God, abstracted from the social and worldly context in which human beings exercise their personhood.

The reductionist character of such a view is obvious. When salvation has to do with something as ethereal as a soul and is restricted in its effects to the isolated, atomic individual, it is evident that we are dealing with an unreal abstraction. Whatever such an experience can mean at the emotional level, it fails to engage the full dynamics of human selfhood in interaction with the concrete realities of the world. Such a shrunken view of salvation touches only peripherally and superficially, if at all, such stubborn forms of bondage as racism, sexism, consumerism, and their institutional objectifications in the social order. This goes a long way toward explaining the strange paradox of the coexistence in many suburban churches of the resurgence of a "born again" Christianity alongside a precipitous decline of Christian social action and concern.

If we are to recover the full implications of the biblical view of salvation, we must see it as a total process of liberation whose dynamics affect all the forms of human bondage—sin, death, law, and the powers. While sin, as we saw in the last chapter, is the basic bondage, it is inextricably linked with the other forms of bondage, both reinforcing them and being reinforced by them. There is no such thing as sin in the abstract. Neither is there any real salvation which does not involve concrete liberations in attitudes, life-styles, relationships, social structures, and institutions. No one has said this better than the Latin American liberation theologian, Gustavo Gutiérrez:

> Sin is basically an alienation, and as such, it cannot be found floating in the air, but is found in concrete historical situations, in individual and specific alienations. It is impossible to understand one without the other. Sin demands a radical liberation, but this, necessarily, includes a liberation in the political order and in the different dimensions of person.[26]

Biblical faith does not bifurcate reality into two self-contained and independent spheres—the religious and the secular, the order of redemption and the order of creation, individual salvation and social transformation. There is a single history of redemption and liberation which involves the whole of the created order. The liberating dynamics of the cross of Christ are simultaneously effective in restoring men and women to communion with God and reconciling them to one another in free community. This means that

> there is no vertical dimension of faith opposed to a horizontal dimension of political love, for in every sphere of life the powers of the coming new creation are in conflict with the powers of a world structure which leads to death. In Christ, God and our neighbour are a unity, and what God has joined together, man shall not put apart, least of all the theologian.[27]

[26] Gustavo Gutiérrez and Richard Shaull, *Liberation and Change,* ed. Ronald H. Stone (Atlanta: John Knox Press, 1977), p. 84.
[27] Moltmann, *The Crucified God,* p. 24.

The seamless robe of Christ's salvation covers both the liberation of the self and the liberation of the sociopolitical structures which are the bones and sinews of human life in society.

Let us look, then, in turn, at the theological dynamics of liberation which are effective in both personal and social salvation. Personal liberation occurs when the bondage of sin is broken by an experience of being grasped by the grace of God mediated through the suffering love of Christ on the cross. Sin, as we have seen, is fed by the anxiety of human beings in the face of their own finitude and death. Their anxiety impels them to either idolatry or apathy—each of them a desperate attempt by persons to contrive their own freedom, meaning, and security on their own terms and at the expense of others. The resultant alienation from God and other human beings leads to an awareness of guilt. Increasingly desperate attempts to deny that guilt through dishonest repression, self-justifying rationalization, and moralistic and legalistic self-salvation only forge more tightly the chains of their bondage.

This whole syndrome of alienation and self-inflicted bondage can be broken through only when the captive self is shattered and reconstituted in confrontation with the judgment and grace mediated by the crucified Christ. In the radical freedom and love of Jesus culminating in his "obedience unto death," our anxious, self-serving attempts to grasp our own freedom at the expense of others is shown up for the self-imposed bondage that it is. At the same time, out of the heart of God's own suffering identification with us in the drama of Calvary, there comes home to us the stunning realization of an unconditional love which affirms us and accepts us in the midst of our alienation and despite our unacceptability. "God shows his love for us in that while we were yet sinners Christ died for us" (Romans 5:8).

The "No" of God's judgment and the "Yes" of his grace, experienced through the cross of Christ, are the liberating dynamics which set us free from the compulsions of the old captive self. No longer do we have to put people down in order to build ourselves up. No longer do we have to mask our real selves behind rationalizations and defensive cover-ups in order to bolster a threatened ego. For this reason, structures of exploitation, domination, and oppression are no longer necessary to establish our identity and maintain our sense of worth. To the extent to which we are liberated from the psychic necessity for these structures, we are no longer blinded and bound by the enslaving ideologies which have been created to justify them. The old master-slave relationship in all its forms—racial prejudice, sexist discrimination, economic exploitation, authoritarian family patterns, etc.—is rendered superfluous by "the freedom with which Christ has set us free."

Christ liberates us to be our true selves by freeing us from the inner compulsions and bondages which distort our humanity. He liberates us by reconstituting our identity as children of God related to him in loving and trustful obedience. He liberates us, also, by making us frce for others, free to be the servants and agents of his ongoing work of liberation in the world. Salvation which does not lead to servanthood is, at best, only a partial and impoverished salvation and, at worst, a contradiction in terms.

The dynamics of liberation of which we have been speaking entail a profound conversion experience—the death of an old self and the birth of a new one. "If any one is in Christ, he is a new creation; the old has passed away, behold, the new has come" (2 Corinthians 5:17). Our revivalistic tradition in America has often trivialized the biblical meaning of conversion to the point where it is no longer a real liberation of consciousness that has radical life-changing consequences. As Herzog says,

> One goes through it [i.e., the rebirth] in a revival, enjoys it, and comes out of it quite unscathed. [But] the change demanded in confrontation with Jesus is something eviscerating, something that touches the core of our being. It destroys the self-made self, that is, man as self-made man. . . . To be freed is always a question of being enabled to identify with the *marginales,* the people on thc borders of society, through the power of the one who started doing it.[28]

A genuine conversion which issues in a true liberation of consciousness will involve a personal decision for Christ. But that decision will include, as an integral part of it, a decision for the neighbor, a decision for Christ's brethren among the poor and the oppressed. To be an effective dynamic for liberation, conversion must also include a commitment to social and political change. The liberated self, the new creation which is the fruit of Christ's redemption, is not a private self, luxuriating in its own inwardness; it is a corporate self committed to the deliverance of the captives.

We have already seen that the liberation of the self from sin has immense ramifications for change in the sociopolitical arena. Anything which neutralizes the power of idolatry and apathy helps to

[28] Herzog, *op. cit.,* pp. 63-64.

weaken the structures of exploitation and oppression and the grip of every enslaving ideology which sanctions them. But to depend on individual conversions alone to break the power of oppressive social structures is unforgivably naive. Such naivete is reflected in the belief of Oscar Cullmann, and shared by many, "that the social question would actually be solved already in this age if every individual would become as radically converted as Jesus demands."[29]

Such a view fails to comprehend the supra-personal demonic forces inherent in social and political objectifications of sin which are not responsive to moral suasion alone. This naive view fails to explain, for example, why racist practices and institutions survived generations of evangelical preaching in the Bible belt and began to crumble only when political and legal power was mobilized against them. The fact is that, as Reinhold Niebuhr never tired of reminding us, love can be made effective in the social sphere only through the creation of political instruments of justice. The oppressions produced by social injustice cannot be dealt with apart from a politics of liberating love.

For the Christian, this involves a vocation of partisanship on behalf of the victims of injustice and oppression. For the church, it involves the abandonment of a posture of neutrality in relation to economic and political realities affecting the poor and the oppressed. The church is called, as Moltmann reminds us, to a double fellowship—a fellowship of believers and a fellowship with and for the poor.[30] We cannot experience his presence in the former without looking for him also in the latter.

Jesus' own partisanship on issues of social and economic justice is unmistakable in the Gospels. It is clear, for example, in the manifesto with which he launched his public mission at Nazareth:

> The Spirit of the Lord is upon me,
> because he has anointed me to preach good news to the poor.
> He has sent me to proclaim release to the captives
> and recovering of sight to the blind,
> to set at liberty those who are oppressed,
> to proclaim the acceptable year of the Lord.
>
> Luke 4:18-19

To be sure, Jesus' partisanship for the poor and the oppressed was not

[29] Oscar Cullmann, *Jesus and the Revolutionaries,* trans. Gareth Putnam (New York: Harper & Row, Publishers, 1970), p. 28.
[30] Moltmann, *The Church in the Power of the Spirit,* pp. 126-129.

an uncritical one. Very little about the kingdom which he was announcing and prefiguring in his own life and ministry could be uncritically identified with any particular liberation movement or with the existing social order. Attempts to make him out as a member of the Zealot revolutionary movement have never been successful, however much he may have sympathized with their cause. For this reason, we must be careful not to use Jesus to baptize uncritically any political movement or policy. The kingdom of freedom which he inaugurated, and which still awaits its final consummation, is not identical with any human, and therefore relative, achievement of liberation.

This eschatological proviso, however, does not justify a stance of neutrality and detachment. Jesus was unquestionably a partisan for the poor and the oppressed. One cannot read the Gospel accounts of his life and teaching and fail to notice his recurring solicitude for the poor coupled with his harsh and stringent criticism of the rich. "Blessed are you poor, for yours is the kingdom of God. But woe to you that are rich, for you have received your consolation" (Luke 6:20*b*, 24). There is no doubt that Jesus took sides. And there is no question about which side he was on.

Does this mean that the affluent suburbanites are beyond the pale of salvation? Not at all. It does mean, however, that, as Jesus said, it is hard for them to enter the kingdom, just as it was hard for Zacchaeus or Dives or the rich young ruler. And two of those three apparently didn't make it. It was not just that for them money had become an ultimate concern—a god. But more than that, their affluence—as is the case also with today's suburbanites—was made possible by the deprivation of the poor. Their affluence could not be separated from the economic inequities and injustices which forged the chains of poverty for others.

Jesus did not take sides with the poor against the rich in order to destroy the latter. He certainly was not interested in simply exchanging the roles of those who were the oppressors and those who were the oppressed. He took sides for the purpose of liberating *both* the rich and the poor, the oppressor *as well as* the oppressed. Liberation for both awaits the elimination of those structures of injustice, domination, and privilege which dehumanize, though in different ways, rich and poor alike. The dynamics of liberation require that we take sides with the oppressed, precisely so that *all* may be liberated, including the oppressor. "Only through the dialectic of taking sides," Moltmann has said, "can the universalism of salvation make its entrance into the world."[31]

The necessity of taking sides in the struggle for liberation poses a special challenge to all those whose calling is to preach to suburban captives. This necessity makes some degree of conflict virtually inevitable in ministry to a suburban congregation. It means that, however pastoral his approach or compassionate his spirit, the minister will be seen by some as the enemy. But this is a cost that must be borne if the church is to be the body of its crucified and risen Lord and the bearer of his gospel of liberation.

[31] Jürgen Moltmann, *Religion, Revolution, and the Future* (New York: Charles Scribner's Sons, 1969), p. 143.

Part Two

Homiletical Strategies

Chapter 3

Communicating the Gospel of Liberation

I n our first chapter, we examined the profile of the suburban captive. We saw how the theological categories descriptive of human bondage help to illumine both the psychological and sociological dimensions of suburban captivity. In chapter 2 we investigated some of the theological dynamics of the Christian message which make it a gospel of liberation, particularly for suburbanites. Our analysis showed, also, how the gospel can be diluted and denatured in ways which rob it of its liberating power and transform it into an ideological support for the social and political status quo.

The discussion thus far has dealt principally with the theological content of the preacher's message as interpreted in relation to the realities of suburban captivity. We are now ready to address more specifically the preaching task itself. In what follows, I will not be dealing with the nuts and bolts of homiletical craftsmanship. Good homiletical manuals abound which are designed to assist the preacher in the techniques of sermon preparation and delivery. My aim, rather, is to offer suggestions concerning a style and strategy for preaching which can enhance the effectiveness of the sermon as an instrument of liberation, especially in the suburban context. The sermons in Part III will provide case studies to illustrate some of the principles and approaches to be discussed in the next two chapters.

In this chapter we will focus primarily on the sermon itself, as we examine certain functional and dynamic elements which are necessary to make the sermon an effective means for communicating the gospel of liberation. The sermon, however, cannot fulfill its liberating potential unless it occurs within a community of faith committed to liberating change in the world. The next chapter will focus on the role of preaching in cultivating and nurturing the church as a community of liberation.

The Sermon as a Liberating Event

What is a sermon? The church has often been bedeviled by a lack of clarity as to what the sermon is and what it is meant to accomplish. What passes for preaching frequently comes across as an erudite lecture or an exercise in moralistic exhortation or a mildly entertaining homily. Sermons have been made to serve duty as promotional pep talks, commentaries on current events, biographical essays, or theological treatises. Preachers have, at various times, seen it as their task to convey information and ideas, to persuade people with logical argument, to advocate a set of moral ideals, or to manipulate the emotions of a congregation with rhetorical eloquence.

In one way or another, all of these notions of what a sermon is about miss the mark. What, then, is the *raison d'etre* of the true sermon? What is it that differentiates the sermon from an essay, lecture, or other forms of communication?

I would contend that *an authentic sermon is essentially a liberating event.* It is an event which occurs between preacher and congregation when the preacher's words become the means by which God makes himself present in liberating efficacy and power. True preaching is always an incarnational happening. When it occurs, the Word of God itself is heard in and through the words of women and men. As Barth puts it, "Preaching is 'God's own Word.' That is to say, through the activity of preaching, God himself speaks."[1]

But God's speaking through the sermon is also a form of doing and acting. The sermon is far more than the transmission of ideas from one mind to another. It is a form of address which, through the recreative power of God's Spirit, engages the total selfhood of the hearer in such a way as to bring about an event of transformation and liberation. "The word of God is alive and active, sharper than any

[1] Karl Barth, *The Preaching of the Gospel,* trans. B. E. Hooke (Philadelphia: The Westminster Press, 1963), pp. 54-55.

double-edged sword. It cuts all the way through, to where soul and
spirit meet, to where joints and marrow come together . . ."
(Hebrews 4:12, TEV). The word of the preacher participates in this
incisive, penetrating action of the Word of God. When it does—that
is, when a true sermon-event or word-event takes place—the defenses
of the captive self are broken through, and a fresh act of God's
liberating grace occurs. The result is a reconstitution and reorienta-
tion of the self in concrete ways—whether through the dissolving of
prejudices or the dispelling of illusions or the reconciling of
relationships. The liberating Word of God mediated through the
word of the preacher puts the hearer in a new situation where old
bondages are broken and new horizons of freedom and fulfillment
are opened up.

The Dramatic Motif in Liberation Preaching

Now it is obvious that not every sermon fulfills its promise of
being a liberating event. Many sermons do little more than inspire
tedium, arouse antipathy, or reinforce apathy. What is it that makes
the difference? What is it that invests preaching with a sense of
urgency? From whence does it derive its passion and its power?
Where do we look for the enabling ingredient that makes the
preacher, again and again, the midwife of "a new birth of freedom" in
the life of his or her hearers?

There are no easy formulas. Certainly it is not a matter of
rhetorical tricks or stylistic refinements in literary craftsmanship. In a
provocative little book, *The Urgency of Preaching,* Kyle Haselden
makes a suggestion that I believe goes to the heart of the matter.
Every good sermon, he says, must have imbedded in its basic
structure the essentials of the divine-human drama of redemption.
This drama appears in the sermon in the form of a recurring motif
which can be schematized as follows: the human peril, the divine
promise, and the catalyst or alterant which moves us from the one to
the other.[2] The same basic theme can be rephrased in the language of
liberation. It would then read: the reality of human bondage and
oppression, the promise of divine liberation, and the liberating
agency of Jesus Christ.

If a sermon is to become a genuinely liberating event, it must
follow a dramatic movement which reflects, in some way, this basic

[2] Kyle Haselden, *The Urgency of Preaching* (New York: Harper & Row, Publishers,
1963), p. 41.

pattern or motif. Needless to say, we are not talking about something that is imposed on the sermon woodenly and artificially from without. We are not proposing the stifling of homiletical creativity by putting the sermon in the straitjacket of a standardized outline. What is at stake here is not a particular form of words—certainly not the unvarying usage of the explicit language of liberation. Indeed, too much use of liberation language would be a stylistic error which might well sound more like a burlesque of reality than an authentically freeing communication of the gospel. Many revivalistic sermons commit this same kind of error with their overly simplistic, sloganizing, and often pedantic repetition of the sin-salvation theme.

More often than not, the bondage-liberation motif will be an implicit rather than an explicit feature of the sermon. But however it may be verbalized—and there can be endless variations of the theme—this dramatic motif provides the inner lifeblood of the sermon which makes it pulse with dynamism and urgency. The sermon which lacks this dramatic tension created by the juxtaposition of the themes of peril and promise, bondage and liberation, may very well be interesting, informative, even edifying. But such a sermon is unlikely to engage the consciousness of the hearer at any profoundly existential level where real liberation can occur. In a word, it leaves the listener cold.

I am suggesting that liberation preaching should follow a pattern that is common to any good dramatic production. A good plot will build a tension between a tragic or a hopeful outcome for the principals in the story. The dramatic suspense is created by the uncertainty instilled in the audience as to whether the possibilities of disaster or fulfillment are finally to prevail. In every play there is a "dramatic hinge" which resolves the tension by swinging the plot decisively in one direction or another, toward tragedy or a happy outcome. It is this resolution of tension through a key movement in the plot which gives the play its emotionally cathartic impact.

The dramatic motif we are discussing is not simply an artificial literary contrivance. It is not a gimmick to give our sermons an aura of drama and suspense. It corresponds to the realities of the human situation as seen in the biblical drama of redemption and liberation. The Deuteronomic covenant of liberation contained both warning and promise, curse and blessing: "I have set before you life and death, blessing and curse; therefore choose life, that you and your descendants may live" (Deuteronomy 30:19b). The new covenant contains the same stark alternatives: "For God so loved the world that he gave his only Son, that whoever believes in him should not perish but have eternal life" (John 3:16).

The biblical message reflects, from beginning to end, this contraposition of the themes of peril and promise, of liberated life over against the threat of bondage and death. It does not, however, leave us dangling indecisively between the two. It proclaims a liberation which is actualized and made effective through the mediating agency of Jesus Christ. "For the Son of God, Jesus Christ," Paul wrote, "was not Yes and No; but in him it is always Yes. For all the promises of God find their Yes in him" (2 Corinthians 1:19-20). But this is not the end of the matter. The "hinge" movement in the drama of liberation includes the "Amen" of human repentance and faith echoing the "Yes" of God's liberating action in Christ. No real liberation occurs till persons are transformed from being mere spectators of the drama to becoming participants in it. Here the preacher must be out for a verdict. The sermon must convey the urgency of summons and invitation, of warning and entreaty. It must aim for something akin to a conversion experience which creates both the agony and the ecstasy of a liberated consciousness.

The dramatic tension of the sermon, far from being contrived, emerges out of the urgency of the gospel itself as it gets communicated through the preacher. Here the preacher's own convictions play an important role. An effective proclamation of the gospel of liberation requires that we feel in our own vitals the urgency of the option we are offering to our people. If we really believe that there is a dynamic in the preached word of the gospel powerful enough to liberate men and women from the most intractable of human bondages, nothing can keep us from preaching, as Samuel Baxter once said, "as a dying man to dying men."

Good News Without Cheap Grace

It takes more, however, than passionate conviction, however authentically inspired by the gospel, to make the sermon a truly liberating event. A great deal depends on *the way* we communicate the reality of human bondage and the promise of divine liberation. The question of how we do this to the best effect raises the issue of the proper relationship between law and gospel, grace and judgment, in our preaching. The crux of the problem is to be heard in such a way that our preaching is received as the Good News of liberation without degenerating into "cheap grace, forgiveness without contrition."

For those of us who preach to suburban captives, this presents a peculiarly difficult challenge. There is a delicate balance to be struck here which makes enormous demands on our powers of empathy and our ability to be sensitive to how our message is being received and decoded by our hearers. There is no way of knowing with certainty whether a particular sermon or text will impact the consciousness of people as law or as gospel. This is, no doubt, what Luther meant when he said, "There's no man living on earth who knows how to distinguish between the law and the gospel. . . . Only the Holy Spirit knows this."[3] Recognition of this limitation, however, does not absolve the preacher from the responsibility of exercising judicious care in seeking to strike a balance between the two. Both law and gospel have an important role to play in preaching "deliverance to the captives." To soft-pedal either at the expense of the other, whether such is done consciously or unconsciously, is to abort the possibilities of liberation.

The Reformers were in agreement that there are at least two uses of the law. One of these is the civil use of the law, which serves to maintain order in society by restraining the unruly impulses stemming from our sinful nature. The other is more directly relevant to the preaching task. This is an essentially propaedeutic use of the law. Such use makes people aware of their sin so that they will be motivated to turn to Christ for help. The law provides a self-revealing mirror which intensifies their consciousness of bondage and guilt to the point where they are ready to turn to God's grace for their deliverance. In this way, the law prepares their hearts for the reception of the gospel.

This use of the law is as essential in preaching to suburban captives as it is in preaching to anyone else. Paradoxically, the word of judgment is a necessary prelude and counterpoint to the experience of liberating grace. Gospel without law is not really good news; it is cheap grace which heals, if it heals at all, only lightly and superficially. A genuinely liberating presentation of the gospel in suburbia will hold up a mirror in which people can see for themselves the false and enslaving elements in their life-style, the subtle ways they exploit others, the masks they wear and the crutches they resort to in order to enhance their self-esteem. Writes Gaylord B. Noyce:

[3] Martin Luther, *Table Talk*, ed. and trans. Theodore G. Tappert, Luther's Works, edited by Helmut T. Lehmann (Philadelphia: Fortress Press, 1967), vol. 54, p. 127

As the cross reminds us, the gospel acknowledges the twistedness of our life, hidden even behind the bland or pleasant suburban countenance. It knows how easily a man can be seduced into thinking that in the backyard swimming pool and the half-acre lot his larger hopes will be fulfilled. The gospel is a word of grace because of this acknowledgment.[4]

In the sermonic case studies in Part Three, there are several examples of preaching which bring the judgment of the gospel to bear on various elements in the suburban ethos, either directly or by implication. The sermon "Our Stewardship of the Earth: Ecology and Faith" links ecology and life-style in a way calculated to raise questions in the mind of the hearer about fundamental values and salvific concerns. "Is it really necessary for our sense of self-importance that we stay in the rat race to keep up with the Joneses?" "Are our lives really so empty, so bereft of meaning, that we have to turn to the latest luxury gadgets and technological toys to relieve our boredom?" "Strangely enough, we cannot separate our stewardship of the earth from the salvation of our souls. When God gets us into a right relationship with himself, he also transforms our relationship with nature—from being nature's predators to becoming nature's caretakers—faithful stewards of the earth."

In an Advent sermon on "Jesus: The Refugee," I attempted to sensitize my congregation to the plight of the world's refugees and their claim on the Christian conscience. Painting a picture of Jesus as a refugee, who still identifies with his fellow-refugees, undoubtedly registered on the consciousness of relatively well-heeled suburbanites as an unsettling preaching of the "law." "If you are a refugee, you are among those who are the unwanted of the world, the rejects of a society which would like to keep you out of sight and out of mind. The refugee, like the rest of the 'invisible poor,' is kept at a distance, in a remote camp somewhere, where he is unable to disturb the slumbering conscience of the rest of us. But no one who truly believes in the Christmas message that God was in Christ reconciling the world unto himself can reject the refugee without being in danger of rejecting Christ himself."

A common pitfall for many preachers is to lay on the members of their congregation a heavy word of judgment and exhortation and then leave them in the dark as to how they might be expected to respond. When preaching fails to provide concrete "handles" for

[4] Gaylord B. Noyce, *The Responsible Suburban Church* (Philadelphia: The Westminster Press, 1970), p. 26.

faithful Christian response and action, the results are not likely to be very liberating. When the sermon provides no road signs to help guide our exodus from captivity, we are left with nothing more than a vague feeling of spiritual malaise or an exacerbated sense of guilt. And unresolved guilt is always an impediment to liberated life and action.

In my view, a good deal of preaching in the sixties which was designed to motivate congregations to social action failed to do so. It failed not because it sounded the note of judgment. That note was an authentic dimension of a much needed prophetic ministry, then as now. The preaching of the sixties failed because its proclamation of judgment was too global, too generalized, too diffuse. Confronted by the pulpit on issues like racism, war, and poverty, which seemed too massive and complex for them to get a handle on, congregations were left feeling confused, frustrated, and guilty. It was natural that their resentment should focus on the minister who put them on a "guilt trip" without providing adequate help in suggesting concrete liberating alternatives for their faith and action.

The refugee problem would seem, on the face of it, to be one of those issues which hardly lends itself to sermonic treatment without courting this very danger. I tried to avoid the pitfall about which I have been speaking by offering, in the conclusion of the sermon, some concrete and feasible options for the congregation's response. Because discussions of the refugee issue had already been initiated among concerned members of the congregation, many people were prepared for my concluding appeal: "I hope that together we may be able to find ways of weaving a web of protection for some of Jesus' fellow-refugees. That might be through sponsoring a refugee family. It might be through exercising political influence to extend our nation's program of refugee resettlement which has virtually ground to a halt. Whatever the specific nature of our response, Jesus will be knocking at our door this Christmas, perhaps in a way more poignant than he has ever done before. If we are going to have him as our Christmas guest, we may have to make room for someone else, too—the one whom he holds by the hand, dressed in the thin and tattered garments of a refugee."

Ideally, no sermon should end when the minister finishes speaking. The word-event which is the sermon should have a continuing history in the experience of the congregants—in an inner and outer dialogue that is carried on after the worship service is over, in commitments that are made and followed through, in learnings and actions which give ongoing life to the preached word. If a sermon does not have this ripple effect, creating a wider history for itself, it must be judged to be stillborn and devoid of liberating consequences.

Only rarely are we given to know how a particular sermon impacts the consciousness of the listener. In this case, it is possible to trace a train of events which followed the sermon, which in turn served as a vehicle for continuing proclamation of the gospel. The sermon was followed by a congregational meeting at which an official decision was made to sponsor a refugee family. The sudden arrival in the parsonage of six refugees from Laos the week before Christmas incarnated, in a very emotional and dramatic way, the meaning of the sermon which had been heard on the previous Sunday. The subsequent encounters between people of radically different cultures, the exposure to the pain and insecurity of just a few of "the wretched of the earth," the fumbling attempts to relate in caring and yet nonoppressive ways—all this added up to a profoundly soul-searching experience for many in the congregation. The sermon "Jesus: The Refugee," as it turned out, was but one episode of a continuing word-event in the life of the congregation. It was one element in a process of motivation and interpretation of a significant event in the church which brought us all under judgment while paradoxically, at the same time, providing an opening for grace.

While our preaching to suburban captives must articulate the judgment of the law if it is to avoid dispensing cheap grace, by itself the law cannot liberate. Only when the imperatives of the law are joined with the gracious indicatives of the gospel can the Good News of liberation really be heard in our preaching. The reason for this is not hard to understand. As T. S. Eliot has observed, "Humankind cannot bear much reality." This is why we resist so tenaciously the revelation of the truth about ourselves which is mirrored in the law. Rather than face the painful truth of our own captivity, we repress it into our subconscious. And our self-imposed blindness to our bondage becomes part of the pathology which afflicts us. As Seward Hiltner has pointed out, "the principal bondages are those not felt as such, or felt so only ambiguously, so that a clear call to change and action is not heard from the conditions themselves. . . . [In fact,] bondage may be perceived clearly only if the person or the group have already begun to emerge from it."[5] Only from a position of

[5] Seward Hiltner, *Theological Dynamics* (Nashville: Abingdon Press, 1972), p. 21.

retrospective security can the reality of past enchainments be seen fully and clearly for what they were.

If this be so, too much preaching of the law which dwells unduly on the conditions of bondage can be an exercise in futility. It may serve only to drive people to an even more desperate reinforcement of their defenses and make them even more dependent on their masks and crutches and legalistic self-justifications in order to cope with the threat to their egos. Clearly what is *not* needed is a moralistic, hortatory style of preaching which majors on accusation and indictment. According to William Hordern, more often than not, that is what people get from their ministers.

> As one listens to the sermons from Protestant pulpits, it becomes clear that the law has replaced the gospel as the central theme. People who go to church have learned to expect that they will be castigated for their sins and that a better way of life will be prescribed to them. They are not often disappointed in these expectations. . . . With the law so central in so much Protestant preaching, it is not surprising that the Protestant laity have come to believe in salvation by works.[6]

Too much preaching of the law only strengthens the enslaving tendencies of self-deception and self-justification. In the final analysis, it is the grace of the gospel and not the chastising of the law which loosens the bonds of our captivity. Until one is made aware at the deepest level of one's being that one is loved and accepted without any conditions, one cannot afford to face the truth about oneself. It is the awesome responsibility of the preacher to sound the note of grace so clearly and convincingly that people are made secure enough to acknowledge their captive condition and begin to participate in their self-liberation.

There are times when the preacher may appropriately pronounce the *woe* of divine judgment on her or his congregation. More characteristically, however, she or he is called to be an instrument of the divine *wooing* of her or his people, mediating to them as winsomely as she or he knows how the unconditional love and forgiveness of God which sets them free. Moltmann correctly identifies the center of gravity of all truly Christian preaching when he says that

> the divine pardon stands at the centre of every proclamation of the gospel, the pardon that liberates men and women from the compulsion

[6] William Hordern, *Living by Grace* (Philadelphia: The Westminster Press, 1975), p. 103.

of evil, from the control of "the powers," from fear of forsakenness, and from the apathy of the empty life, and that gives them courage for a new life for the kingdom in fellowship with Christ.[7]

Among the sermons in Part Three, there are two in particular which articulate in different ways the reality of grace as a liberating dynamic in human experience: "Free Indeed: Our Gospel of Liberation" and "The God Who Won't Give Up on Us." It is obvious, on reading these sermons, that they deal thematically with grace. One should not jump too quickly from this observation to the conclusion that they, in fact, mediated grace to the hearer. To do so would be to be confused about what Leander E. Keck refers to as "the difference between communicating grace and advocating a concept called grace."[8]

> Actually, one should preach so that a new situation is created for the hearer, one in which he is grasped by grace.
>
> A grace-event occurs when the word about Jesus reaches the hearer as good news for him; or, to put it in different terms, in hearing the word about Jesus something decisive can occur which can liberate and reorient the hearer.[9]

This certainly was part of the intention of the preacher in the preparation and delivery of these sermons. But Luther's caution about not being able to distinguish between law and gospel should give us pause when we try to assess the degree to which my sermons were actually received as Good News and provided the occasion for a liberating grace-event. Despite his or her best intentions and most arduous efforts, the preacher is often disappointed. The sermon "The God Who Won't Give Up on Us" was prepared in the wake of a complaint from one of my members that he felt judged and put down by my preaching. In responding to such a criticism, it is vital that the minister strive for a sense of balance and perspective. His or her reaction should be neither defensive nor overly deferential. The criticism may reflect a healthy awakening of conscience in response to an authentic but painful communication of the judgment of God on the person's life. It may come from the desire of the aroused conscience to receive cheap grace. On the other hand, the criticism

---

[7] Jürgen Moltmann, *The Church in the Power of the Spirit,* trans. Margaret Kohl (New York: Harper & Row, Publishers, 1977), p. 223.

[8] Leander E. Keck, *A Future for the Historical Jesus* (Nashville: Abingdon Press, 1971), p. 102.

[9] *Ibid.*

may suggest to the minister the need for adjusting the balance between law and gospel in his preaching so that the note of grace comes through more distinctly. It may be symptomatic of a tender conscience suffering an overload of law.

At any rate, the sermon in question represents the fruit of just this kind of ministerial soul searching. I used the parables of the lost sheep and the lost coin to portray the persistence and tenacity of the love of God which refuses to give up on us even when we give up on ourselves and on one another. I deliberately resisted the temptation to dramatize and dwell on the condition of human lostness and sin which many sermons on these parables have emphasized. In another situation or at another time this approach might well have been valid. But it did not seem appropriate here. In every congregation, there are a goodly number of people whose self-image is very low and who already feel "put down" and under judgment. "What if you are a sinner, and you don't need anyone to tell you that you are? What if you are lost, and no one knows it better than you?" The sermon was designed with folks like this particularly in mind. The word that needed articulation at this moment, it seemed to me, was a nonjudgmental word of unconditional acceptance and grace. "God doesn't demand that we shape up or ship out. He isn't in the business of keeping moral scorecards and striking balance sheets. The only trip he lays on us is a love that will not let us go, a love that keeps searching us out and calling us home."

In some circumstances, such a message might be thought to encourage the notion of cheap grace. Knowing the situation and the people to whom it was addressed, my guess is that, for the most part, the message registered otherwise. In any case, the love that will not let us go makes its own kind of demands on us which may be even more rigorous than the legalistic demands of a works-righteousness. And those who are out for cheap grace will be as uncomfortable in the presence of such love as they are under the scrutiny of the law.

When all is said and done, we preachers have no guarantees that we will be on target. We will try to be as sensitive as possible to where people are in their need for a particular word of judgment or of grace. But since so much depends on what the listener brings to the preaching event, we cannot predict or control what responses we will get. With respect to our preaching, as in other matters, we preachers are ourselves justified by grace. This awareness can be immensely freeing. If we are not hung up on the need always to succeed in our preaching, we can be a great deal more sensitive and responsive to the real needs of our people. If we can trust the outcome to God, we can be more effective servants of the liberating word. If we do not have to justify ourselves in our own eyes or in the eyes of our people, we can be bearers of Good News without cheap grace.

Preaching as Consciousness Raising

Our theological analysis in the earlier part of this book revealed that one of the basic elements in the structure of suburban captivity is a largely unconscious enslavement to false myths and ideologies which distort one's perception of reality. Because this enslavement is, in the main, unconscious rather than conscious, it does not yield to objective rational argument or direct moral appeal. Such an approach is apt to lead only to more desperate rationalizations of oppressive behavior patterns and more compulsive clinging to mythical interpretations of reality which reinforce the captive ego's defenses. The fanaticism and fury of the backlash which has followed the exposure, in recent years, of the racist and sexist assumptions endemic to our society demonstrate the impotence of a too simple moral and rational approach to the problem.

What is needed is a process of consciousness raising akin to the biblical experience of conversion which breaks the demonic spell of the false myths which hold people captive. The captive self must be freed up to the point where it is able to see reality in a new light, where it is able to let go of the comfortable but distorting illusions which seemed so necessary for its integrity and self-preservation. This kind of consciousness raising provides such a radically new way of seeing the self and its world that the biblical imagery of the "new birth" seems an entirely appropriate way of describing it.

Characteristic New Testament images of conversion depict a transition from darkness to light, from blindness to seeing, which is descriptive also of a process of consciousness raising. These images figure prominently, for example, in the conversion of Saul, the arch oppressor of the Christian community, to Paul, the apostle of freedom. Following his encounter on the Damascus road with a light brighter than the sun, he receives this mandate for his ministry to the Gentiles: "I send you to open their eyes and turn them from darkness to light, and from the dominion of Satan to God . . ." (Acts 26:18, NEB). This same mandate is laid on every preacher of the gospel—to remove the scales of blindness from people's eyes and to lead them to a new mode of consciousness, a new way of seeing—to make them conscious of their bondage to a mythical world of idols and to turn them to the possibilities of liberated existence which God in Christ has opened up for them.

Every act of preaching which is faithful to the gospel carries with it the potential for consciousness raising by virtue of the very nature of the message which is proclaimed. "The annunciation of the Gospel," insists Gustavo Gutiérrez, "has a conscienticizing function, or in other words, a politicizing function." [10] The kinds of dynamics which are set in motion by the proclamation of the gospel are described by him in these words:

> If a situation of injustice and exploitation is incompatible with the coming of the Kingdom, the Word which announces this coming ought normally to point out this incompatibility. This means that the people who hear this message and live in these conditions by the mere fact of hearing it should perceive themselves as oppressed and feel impelled to seek their own liberation. Very concretely, they should "feel their hunger" and become aware that this hunger is due to a situation which the Gospel repudiates. [11]

This description, of course, fits the situation of oppressed people in the Third World better than the particular form of human bondage to be found in a typical suburban congregation. In both situations, however, the proclamation of the gospel is capable of unveiling the dehumanizing contradictions of personal and social reality and motivating people to desire and work for their own liberation and that of others. Whether those who hear the proclamation fit mainly in the category of the oppressed or the oppressor, in either case their consciousness is burdened with a false and distorted perception of reality. "One of the gravest obstacles to the achievement of liberation," Paulo Freire writes, "is that oppressive reality absorbs those within it and thereby acts to submerge men's consciousness." [12]

This is true for oppressors and oppressed alike, both of whom are unable to see the prevailing situation of oppression as anything but normative and inevitable. What is needed is a liberation of the consciousness which breaks the grip of this false perception of reality

---

[10] Gustavo Gutiérrez, *A Theology of Liberation* (Maryknoll, N.Y.: Orbis Books, 1973), p. 269.

[11] *Ibid.*

[12] Paulo Freire, *Pedagogy of the Oppressed,* trans. Myra Bergman Ramos (New York: The Seabury Press, Inc., 1970), p. 36. Copyright © 1970 by Paulo Freire. Used by permission of Seabury Press, Inc.

and enables the person to see that the reality of oppression is neither a necessary nor justifiable part of the scheme of things. "In order for the oppressed to be able to wage the struggle for their liberation, they must perceive the reality of oppression not as a closed world from which there is no exit, but as a limiting situation which they can transform."[13] Such a perception flows naturally from the proclamation of the gospel. Its liberating announcement is that Christ has undermined the regency of every oppressive power and thrown open the doors of every prison so that we can go free.

Freire has developed an educational methodology which applies the consciousness-raising approach to the particular needs of the oppressed peoples of the Third World. His method of "conscientization," originally designed for the poverty-stricken and illiterate peasants of Brazil, has provided a model for many liberation movements throughout the world, including the women's movement in our own country.[14] While there are obvious limits to its applicability to the North American suburban scene, certain features of Freire's model can illuminate the way in which preaching in suburbia can serve a consciousness-raising function.

Before proceeding to make these applications, however, it may be necessary to justify this use of insights from a "pedagogy of the oppressed" in the liberation of those who are perceived by many to be oppressors. Some would say that such an attempt is bound to blur the distinction between oppressor and oppressed, a distinction which must be insisted on, at all costs, until the oppressor is forced to surrender his position of domination and privilege. After all, conscientization is a way of arousing the oppressed from their torpor and mobilizing them for revolutionary action against the systems which oppress them. How could it possibly be a relevant approach to privileged suburbanites whose very way of life is made possible, at least in part, by the maintenance of structures of injustice and oppression?

Here we need to be careful that we do not fall into the mistake of using categories which fail to take account of the complexities and ambiguities of suburban captivity. As we pointed out earlier, the oppressed-oppressor distinction is a relative rather than an absolute one. It is as misleading to say that all suburbanites are equally guilty

---

[13] *Ibid.,* p. 34.

[14] Cf. Letty M. Russell, *Human Liberation in a Feminist Perspective—A Theology* (Philadelphia: The Westminster Press, 1974), chapter 4.

of being oppressors as it is to say that all inner-city minorities are simply innocent victims of oppression. No doubt, all of us who live in suburbia are implicated in supporting structures of oppression, whether we realize it or not. Part of the task of the consciousness-raising process is to enable us to recognize the uncomfortable truth that we do, in fact, oppress our fellow human beings, systemically if not individually, and to begin to take responsibility for that fact.

The other side of the coin is that in various ways suburbanites are themselves oppressed as well as being oppressors. This is not to say that oppression weighs on them anything like it does, for example, on the disadvantaged minorities in the ghettos and barrios of our cities. Nor does it deny what we have been emphasizing all along—that a large part of the bondage of suburban captivity is self-inflicted, a consequence of sinful idolatry and the abuse of human freedom. But if oppression is defined as the diminishing of one's freedom and humanity by human agencies and forces which violate and manipulate our personhood, who is to say that the suburbanite is not also oppressed in very real ways?

Naive romanticism or neurotic alienation may prompt us to want to deny this fact. But a healthy love for our parishioners should engender a real sensitivity to the ways in which they are trapped and victimized by institutional and ideological forces which circumscribe their freedom to be fully human. We need to be able to empathize with the dilemmas of the executive caught in the grind of having to show adequate profit margins, sometimes by going along with corporate decisions which fail to measure up to his or her own personal standards of justice and decency. We need to be able to understand the frustrations of the employee who is bypassed for promotion because of the requirements of an affirmative action policy in his company. We need to be aware of the sense of entrapment experienced by the suburban housewife which can turn her into a nagging wife or an obsessive mother.

In addition to such imprisonment by social and occupational roles, suburbanites share today the general sense of impotence in the face of our mass bureaucratic and technological society. They do not see their voices counting for much, if anything. They have a sense of their destiny being determined for them. All too many have succumbed to the "you can't fight city hall" syndrome. The kind of fatalism which Freire found among Brazilian peasants which reduced them to what he calls a "culture of silence" is not by any means absent from suburbia. Moreover, commercial interests using the power of the mass media have brainwashed suburbanites into confusing real happiness and fulfillment with a constantly escalating standard of living. The pressures from these artificially induced needs and desires weigh oppressively on people in suburbia as in other parts of our society. While the rat race to keep up with the Joneses is, in part, an expression of personal selfishness and greed, it is also the result of our subtle manipulation by economic forces in ways of which we are often not even aware. Thus do the principalities and powers of this world oppressively reinforce our individual propensities for evil.

This brief excursus has shown that suburbanites are caught in a web of oppressive reality which makes it difficult to determine whether they are more the oppressors than the oppressed or more sinned against than sinning. What is clear is the need for a heightened consciousness of the ways in which they are oppressed and in which they oppress others which will lead to a commitment to act against the realities of oppression. To the degree to which our preaching contributes to a more critical awareness of the dehumanizing contradictions under which people live and motivates them to liberating action, it serves as an instrument of conscientization.

A sermon which I preached on Father's Day entitled "On Being a Man" was just such an exercise in consciousness raising aimed at the chauvinistic images of manhood so prevalent in our culture. "Men in our culture," I said in the introduction to the sermon, "are victimized by certain images of themselves, certain notions of what it takes really to be a man, which add up to a form of bondage. Distorted images of masculinity drive men compulsively to 'prove their manhood' in ways which take a terrible toll in frustration and destructiveness."

The sermon went on to analyze the "Archie Bunker syndrome." It tried to point out, with the aid of "All in the Family" episodes and the biblical story of the Fall, the way in which this distorted view of maleness leads to self-deception and oppression of others, to "operation cover-up" and "operation put-down." The sermon concluded by lifting up the contrasting image of true manhood which we encounter in Jesus and a reminder of the liberating grace of God which frees us from the necessity to prove our manhood.

The response to the sermon indicated a variable measure of success in achieving my consciousness-raising objective. On the one hand, there was an angry reaction from one man who resented what he saw to be a debunking of a favorite folk hero. On the other hand, a successful businessman confessed that the sermon had provided a mirror in which he was able to see some things about himself which left him very disturbed. One might judge, perhaps, that this represented at least some movement toward liberation. Several women, incidentally, were quick to catch the implications of the sermon for their own liberation from male chauvinism.

As Freire describes it, there are at least three important and interrelated elements in the conscientizing process: (1) Central to the process is dialogical encounter. (2) The dialogue, however, is not about abstract ideas but is focused on concrete images or themes which reflect the real world of personal and social reality. (3) The aim of the dialogue is to move from a naive to a criticial consciousness of self and world which issues in liberating action to change the world. The essence of the method is summarized by Freire in these words: "Dialogue is the encounter between men, mediated by the world, in order to name the world. . . . Dialogue is the encounter in which the united reflection and action of the dialoguers are addressed to the world which is to be transformed and humanized. . . ."[15]

This method suggests three ingredients for a conscientizing style of preaching. It must be dialogical; it must use concrete images to mediate the reality of the world in the light of the gospel; and it must be related closely to the liberating praxis of the Christian community. It should be obvious that such a style of preaching can be meaningful and effective only in the context of a dialogical or covenant community with a commitment to a mission of liberation. For this reason, I will discuss these matters in a separate chapter devoted to ways in which such a community of liberation can be cultivated within the church.

[15] Freire, *op. cit.*, pp. 76-77.

Chapter 4

Cultivating a Community of Liberation

I n the last chapter, the sermon was defined as essentially a liberating event. It is important now to emphasize that its effectiveness as an instrument of liberation depends very largely on the personal and communal context in which it occurs. Indeed, if this context for preaching is lacking, much of the content of our message, however liberating its potential may be, will be lost on our hearers.

The Communal Context of Liberation Preaching

H. H. Farmer underscored the importance of the context of preaching a number of years ago in his little classic on preaching, *The Servant of the Word.* "The act of preaching," he wrote, "is part of a larger system of personal relationships and cannot be rightly understood in separation from it. The preacher, his sermon and his hearers are embedded in this larger system, and what the preaching effects largely depends upon it." [1]

An obvious corollary of this relationship is that preaching, to be effective, must rise out of and be informed by a sensitive, ongoing pastoral ministry. It is almost a truism to say that it takes a good pastor to be a good preacher. George Buttrick was surely right when he wrote, "Only the pastor, or a man with pastoral imagination, can

[1] Herbert H. Farmer, *The Servant of the Word* (New York: Charles Scribner's Sons, 1942), p. 93.

77

preach."[2] If we fail to forge relationships of love and trust with our people through our pastoral activity, our preaching inevitably "takes on the brassiness which the Apostle said characterises even the speech of angels when there is no love."[3]

The other side of the coin, however, is equally true. An unresponsive, apathetic congregation, with no real sense of identity as a community of faith and mission, can vitiate and neutralize what might otherwise be intrinsically good preaching. "It is not only lovelessness on the part of the preacher," says Farmer, "that turns him into a sounding brass and a tinkling cymbal. It is lovelessness in the church, for preaching is an act of the church. 'I cannot hear what you say, because what the congregation is shouts so loud.'"[4]

Thus, it is clear that the act of preaching and the community of the church exist together in a symbiotic relationship, each being essential to the other for its proper functioning. Vital preaching does not grow in a vacuum. Preaching is not a virtuoso solo performance, even if the responsibility for proclamation is largely vested in a single individual. "The proclamation of the gospel always belongs within a community, for every language lives in a community or creates one."[5] Liberating preaching, as a rule, can take place only where people are in the process of being liberated and being formed into a community of liberation. Preaching is the indispensable activity in the church which serves to focalize that process and contribute to the formation and nurture of that community.

Preaching is a form of communication which involves more than a word addressed to individuals who happen to be gathered together in one place. Its primary meaning and purpose derive from the fact that it is an integral part of an act of public worship. As such, preaching is the corporate activity of a community of faith trying to get its bearings and define its identity and mission with reference to the gospel of Christ which gives it its reason for being. Two correspondences are necessary to provide the context in which real preaching—preaching that has liberating consequences—can occur. On the one hand, the gospel as preached, the word as articulated in the sermon, must correspond with and faithfully reflect the story of

[2] George Arthur Buttrick, *Sermons Preached in a University Church* (Nashville: Abingdon Press, 1959), p. 7.

[3] Farmer, *op. cit.,* p. 94.

[4] *Ibid.,* p. 99.

[5] Jürgen Moltmann, *The Church in the Power of the Spirit,* trans. Margaret Kohl (New York: Harper & Row, Publishers, 1977), p. 224.

God's liberating action for us in Jesus Christ, his incarnate Word. On the other hand, there must be some recognizable correspondence between a worshiping and witnessing congregation and the gospel. When these two correspondences are established, preaching can again and again be the means of "a new birth of freedom."

The Liberating Fellowship and the Servanthood of the Liberated

Moltmann summarizes the essential character of the community which flows naturally from an authentic proclamation of the gospel and which, in turn, makes that proclamation a continuing possibility:

> The fellowship which corresponds to the gospel in its original interpretation is the messianic community. It is the fellowship which narrates the story of Christ, and its own story with that story, because its own existence, fellowship and activity springs from that story of liberation. It is a "story-telling fellowship," which continually wins its own freedom from the stories and myths of the society in which it lives. from the present realization of this story of Christ.[6]

As a messianic community, the church is called to be a sign and prototype of God's promised kingdom of freedom. It constitutes a zone of freedom where the powers of God's promised future begin to take effect in the world now. In the midst of a world of repression and alienation, a world captive to sin, death, law, and the powers, the church represents the presence of incarnate hope. By providing anticipatory tokens of the new humanity already embodied in Christ, it points to a new future of freedom for the world. By doing, as well as telling, God's freedom story, the church can infect the world with the contagion of liberating hope.

The creation and cultivation of such a community of liberation is dependent, more than anything else, on a faithful preaching of the gospel. As Moltmann reminds us, "It is not the church that has the gospel; it is the gospel that creates for itself a people of the exodus, which is the true church of Christ."[7] This is why its kerygmatic character, as a storytelling fellowship, is foundational to the church's true being. The retelling and reenactment of the gospel story in contemporary terms draw the church into God's own history of liberation. Since preaching lies at the heart of the storytelling process, it can in no way be regarded as an optional or peripheral activity in the life of the church. It is, in fact, strategically essential to the

---

[6] *Ibid.*, p. 225.
[7] *Ibid.*, p. 84.

ongoing formation of the church as a liberated people of God.

Preaching should aim at building up the church both as *koinonia* and as *diakonia.* These two are mutually interdependent aspects of the being of the church which must be cultivated simultaneously, if the church is to become and remain a community of liberation.

As *koinonia,* the church is a liberating fellowship and a fellowship of the liberated. True liberation is never a purely individualistic achievement. It grows out of a sharing of words, meanings, emotions, and actions in a fellowship of mutual love and trust. Wherever the church is an intentional community seeking to realize the presence of Christ in its midst, such a fellowship becomes a possibility. Within such a fellowship, characterized by mutual acceptance and affirmation, people are encouraged to drop their masks and let go of their crutches. They find it less necessary to resort to "cover-up" or "put-down" techniques to assure themselves of their own worth; for within the Christian fellowship they already know themselves to be important and significant in the sight of God and of one another. Moreover, by finding a new identity through sharing their faith and hope in Christ, they begin to be emancipated from the enslaving myths and compulsive behavior patterns of the wider society.

Whenever the ferment of the gospel produces a fellowship of the liberated, a new social organism emerges which reflects in its concrete existence visible marks of the liberated life. The church is never truly the church until some such visible signs of newness are present in its corporate and institutional life. In the church's *koinonia* the old divisions and conflicts based on race, sex, wealth, power, and privilege lose their force and validity. "There is neither Jew nor Greek, there is neither slave nor free, there is neither male nor female; for you are all one in Christ Jesus" (Galatians 3:28).

If the church is a society in which that kind of mandate is in effect, clearly no one can pull rank on anyone else. Patterns of domination and dependency which define the rules of the game in the world at large are out of place here. Exploitive uses of power, whether crass or subtle, represent a denial of Christian fellowship. So also does the exclusion of women from leadership roles, the domination of the laity by the clergy, or the concentration of decision making in the church in the hands of its more economically privileged members.

Within the Christian fellowship every member has an equal dignity and an equal voice as he or she participates in the "priesthood of all believers." All have the gift of the Spirit and, hence, both the freedom and responsibility to share fully in shaping the direction of the church's life as a fellowship of the Spirit. All have unique gifts of ministry. And it is the task of the *koinonia* to assist the individual in discovering and expressing these gifts for the common good. Without such presuppositions of equality of personal dignity and capacity for ministry, any profession of being a fellowship of the liberated is bound to be more fictitious than real.

Every achievement of real *koinonia,* however ambiguous it may be, represents a breakthrough for human liberation. It is a breach, however small, in the wall of dehumanizing and oppressive forces of a society which makes it difficult for us to maintain our humanness. Because it *is* such a precious achievement, the church has often seen fit to channel its efforts almost exclusively in this direction. It has been busy creating pockets of *koinonia* here and there to insulate men and women from the dehumanizing and depersonalizing influences of the world. But it has done little to challenge or change the oppressive social structures and ideologies from which these influences emanate.

What has happened is that churches have tended to major on *koinonia* at the expense of their *diakonia.* But a concept of church which is all *koinonia* and no *diakonia* is a heretical one which aborts the church's mission of liberation to the oppressed as mandated by the gospel. It leads to heretical structures—forms of organization which turn the church in upon itself rather than outward in servanthood to the world. When this happens, people are encouraged to indulge in dreams of liberation in an alienated form. Such alienated dreams can poison the springs of *koinonia* itself. For when the church does not reach out beyond itself in loving service to and solidarity with the poor and the oppressed, the Christian authenticity of its own fellowship is called into question. Simply to luxuriate in one's own experiences of freedom while others are still in chains is, in a profound sense, to be estranged from one's true humanity. Such freedom is bound to be something less than the full-orbed freedom promised in the gospel, which in Christ has been defined for us—not just as "the freedom to be," but "the freedom to be for others."

In his book on *Liberation in Middle America,* Gabriel J. Fackre describes the way in which the churches during the religious revival of the fifties courted this alienated dream of liberation:

Institutional religion provided John Doe a chance to get back his name and his face, albeit within a very limited sector of his culture. In the lay-oriented and grass-roots style of American church life—although it frequently trivialized its participatory democracy . . . —people did experience some control over their future. And further, within its caring community—the concept of koinonia, fellowship, ranked higher as a priority in the church of the fifties—there was provided a buffer against the depersonalizing current in the wider world.[8]

This banding together to create islands of freedom and cohumanity in the midst of a repressive society is understandable and, up to a point, liberating. But when the goal of *koinonia* is embraced to the exclusion of *diakonia,* we end up with a truncated version of the biblical vision of liberation. That vision, as we have seen, encompasses the defeat of the principalities and powers of this world as well as inward redemption from sin. And, as Fackre reminds us, "The quest for a utopia on the margins of society aborts the major task of building social structures which embody that mirror for all the hopes of liberation and reconciliation."[9]

If the search for liberation in spiritual inwardness and social intimacy was the temptation of the institutional Christianity of the fifties, it would seem that this trend is even more powerful in the seventies. After a short-lived period of social activism in the sixties, churches are again turning inward. Pietism is again being substituted for servanthood. Strong waves of evangelicalism are sweeping the suburbs of our nation, and "born again" Christianity is becoming almost fashionable among middle-class types.

That there are real signs of vitality in this new outburst of religious fervor and energy cannot be denied. But there is also the danger that the spiritual dynamism of this movement, which could have salutary effects for human liberation if turned outward, will be bottled up and wasted in an inward-looking spirituality. The challenge of preaching at this juncture of our history is to turn these alienated dreams of liberation outward. Its task is to harness the energies released by the evangelical experience of grace for the liberation of those who suffer from oppressive social structures. To accomplish this task, preaching must work at the creation and nurture of a style of Christian community which embodies *diakonia* as well as *koinonia*—the servanthood of the liberated as well as a fellowship which liberates.

[8] Gabriel J. Fackre, *Liberation in Middle America* (Philadelphia: Pilgrim Press, 1971), p. 37.

[9] *Ibid.*

Dialogical Preaching and Liberation

We can be helped in this undertaking, I believe, by borrowing some clues from Freire's method of conscientization and adapting them to the exigencies of the preaching task. Simply stated, conscientization is a method of dialogical action designed to encourage the participants in the dialogue (in this case, the preacher and the congregation) to reflect critically on a shared experience of concrete reality with a view to changing it. Dialogical communication is the crucial factor in unveiling the contradictory and oppressive character of existing reality and motivating people for liberating action to transform that reality.

If dialogue is essential to consciousness-raising and liberating praxis, it would appear that preaching is an unlikely candidate to bear the weight of this mode of communication. Indeed, according to the conventional image, preaching is anything but dialogical. The feeling that many people have that they are being "preached at" when the minister mounts the pulpit confirms the stereotype that preaching is essentially monological. The very physical arrangement of a raised pulpit seems to suggest that the preacher is six feet above contradiction and that the Word as preached is removed from the common life of the people and made the preacher's exclusive prerogative.

Reuel Howe comments on the way in which this conventional style of preaching frustrates the possibility of much real communication:

> Conventional preaching . . . is largely "one way" or monological in its concept of communication. It has become locked up in a stereotype that stifles the potential creativity of every preacher. This "performer" image of preaching, which is the name of the stereotype, throttles the potential power of preaching. The purpose of communication is to produce a meeting of meaning from two sides. Monologue, however, is concerned only with the imposition of meaning from one side.[10]

When the monological style dominates in preaching, the congregation tends to be reduced to passivity and irresponsibility. It becomes an audience of people who expect to be inspired, entertained, or have their thinking done for them. When this is what people are conditioned to expect from preaching, the preacher should not be

[10] Reuel L. Howe, *Partners in Preaching: Clergy and Laity in Dialogue* (New York: The Seabury Press, Inc., 1967), p. 34. Copyright © 1967 by The Seabury Press, Inc. Used by permission of The Seabury Press, Inc.

surprised at the stereotypical response he receives at the door of the sanctuary: "Pastor, I enjoyed your sermon this morning."

This monological approach to preaching not only reduces the possibilities of real communication; it encourages a relationship between preacher and congregation which is oppressive rather than liberating. It is analogous to what Freire calls the "banking" concept of education. "Education thus becomes an act of depositing, in which the students are the depositories and the teacher is the depositor. Instead of communicating, the teacher issues communiqués and makes deposits which the students patiently receive, memorize, and repeat."[11] This banking method of education is a ready instrument of oppression. It neutralizes the creativity of students, stimulates their credulity, and renders them docile and acquiescent in the face of the systems which oppress them.

It is dreadfully easy for preaching to become antidialogical and oppressive in the same way as education. Paternalistic assumptions and attitudes readily intrude into our preaching, often in ways of which we are not conscious. Lay persons can easily be intimidated by the feeling that we do, in fact, regard them as empty vessels waiting to be filled by our superior store of divinely inspired wisdom. When we fail to respect the experiences and insights of lay people and our sermons regularly bypass the urgent, but unarticulated, questions which the people bring with them, they are bound to feel oppressed by their concerns, even though they may seldom muster the courage to express how they really feel. No doubt, a good deal of resistance to preaching, as well as outright anticlerical resentment, stems from this feeling of being dominated and negated in an essentially one-sided process of communication.

All of this can be remedied only when we train ourselves to practice a dialogical style of preaching. But how can preaching be dialogical when, by its very nature, a sermon is a monologue with only one person doing the speaking? Reuel Howe reminds us that the sermon, though formally a monologue, can be governed by the dialogical principle in its preparation, delivery, and content.

> When the dialogical principle governs a communication, the speaker feels responsible for and responds to the patterns of experience and understanding that his listener brings to the situation, and thus the listener is encouraged to grapple with his own meaning in relation to the

[11] Paulo Freire, *Pedagogy of the Oppressed* (New York: The Seabury Press, Inc., 1970), p. 58.

speaker's meaning. . . . He experiences an invitation to participate even though at the moment he cannot speak aloud. But because he is addressed dialogically, he will speak and act later.[12]

The dialogical approach to preaching becomes particularly important when the objective of preaching is to activate a congregation to its servanthood in the world and nurture people in their own ministries of liberation. If the minister is to "equip the saints for the work of ministry" (Ephesians 4:12a), he or she must find ways of including them in the partnership of preaching. Sermons must address the concrete context of their ministries in the world. They must stimulate a dialogue between the Word of God and the problems, issues, and resistances which they encounter in their worldly mission. They must contribute to the building of "sermons" which lay persons themselves are preaching as part of their liberating praxis in places of secular responsibility.

For preaching to be vitally dialogical, it is just as important that ministers be sensitive listeners as it is that they be skillful speakers. They must find ways of creating feedback networks so that they can be in touch not only with the verbal responses of lay people but also with sometimes hidden agendas which lie behind their responses. Study groups, vocational support groups, issue forums, and sermon seminars all provide "listening posts" to enhance the preachers' awareness of where lay persons are coming from and how they are understanding and relating the gospel to their daily lives. Without some such feedback, ministers are flying blind in their preaching. One pole of the dialogue is being suppressed. As a result, the preached Word fails to make the critical connections with the concrete situations of life faced by the lay persons where its liberating potential can be released.

The aim of preaching should be to foster a dialogical community in which people are helped to reflect meaningfully and critically on the concrete issues raised by their mission in the world. During a recent Lenten season, our church engaged in an experiment in dialogue designed to further this objective. A Sunday evening series of small-group discussions were held concurrently with a Sunday morning sermon series on "The Gospel and the Church." In these sermons, I attempted to expound the biblical-theological bases for understanding the church as both *koinonia* and *diakonia*. Prior to

[12] Howe, *op. cit.*, pp. 47-48.

each sermon and discussion, members were provided with a list of Scripture readings out of which the sermons were built and a brief study guide with questions to focus their discussions. Through this linkage of sermon and discussion, the congregation experienced a new sense of the dialogical nature of a covenant community. The same format can be used with any number of topical areas to help lay persons, through dialogical sharing, to shape their own sermon to the world in word and action.

One more thing must be said in relation to dialogical preaching and the liberation process which is particularly important in the suburban setting. The circle of those included in the dialogue must be drawn wide enough to include the silent voices of the poor and the oppressed in the conversation. The minister must take the lead in insuring that they get an adequate hearing by playing the role of the advocate on their behalf. If the exclusive circles of suburban *koinonia* are to be broken open and the servanthood of the liberated made a reality, someone must introduce into the ongoing dialogue of the church a concern for "the wretched of the earth." The church's dialogue is bound to be inauthentic and alienating if the interests of the victimized and outcasts of society are not somehow represented in it. It will be alienated not only from the real world but from the gospel and from Christ as well.

The minister may hesitate to enlarge the scope of the church's dialogue in this way for fear of endangering communication with many of the people in the congregation. This is a consideration not to be taken lightly, for no minister should play fast and loose with the trust and confidence of a congregation. At the same time, we need to feel the force of some rhetorical questions posed by Kyle Haselden in relation to this matter:

> Is the minister's duty limited to those who belong to his church and pay its bills? Is he not also sent to "the lost sheep of the house of Israel," to the gentiles who ask only for the crumbs beneath the table? He may have a contract which binds him to some people, but he is under a covenant which binds him to all people. The poor, the brokenhearted, the captives, the blind, the bruised—must he not under that covenant maintain communication with *them?*[13]

Indeed, he must! And he must also keep open his communication with the remnant in his own congregation who are sufficiently

---

[13] Kyle Haselden, *The Urgency of Preaching* (New York: Harper & Row, Publishers, 1963), p. 83.

liberated to begin to assume the risks of expressing their solidarity with the oppressed in word and deed. The minister cannot always be all things to all people. There comes a time when urgent issues are joined, when the minister must risk breaking the dialogue with some in order to stand with those who are venturing forth courageously in Christ's liberating mission in the world. Such choices are never easy. They involve us in negotiating what must always be an uneasy balance between prophetic partisanship and pastoral sensitivity.

Relating Preaching and Praxis

It should be evident from the foregoing discussion why the dialogical dimension is so important in our preaching. It is not a matter of engaging in dialogue just for the sake of dialogue. Nor is dialogue simply a tool for "getting our ideas across" in a more persuasive fashion. If the exchange that occurs in the preaching event is at the level of ideas only, genuine dialogue has not yet been achieved. Real dialogue is an encounter between men and women which includes both reflection and action. It is, as Freire describes it, an encounter which frees people to act as true subjects capable of saying their own word to the world, "naming" it, and taking action to change it. Seen in this way, dialogue is inseparable from a liberating praxis. "There is no true word that is not at the same time a praxis. Thus, to speak a true word is to transform the world." [14]

If *koinonia* without *diakonia* does not create a true church, then preaching that is not related to liberating action does not communicate a true word. What Freire says about the use of words in general applies *a fortiori* to the word of preaching.

> When a word is deprived of its dimension of action, reflection automatically suffers as well; and the word is changed into idle chatter, into *verbalism,* into an alienated and alienating "blah." It becomes an empty word, one which cannot denounce the world, for denunciation is impossible without a commitment to transform, and there is no transformation without action. [15]

The reason why so much preaching lacks power is that it suffers from just this kind of vacuous verbalism. The preacher's words are empty and sterile when they do not "mean" or "intend" action that liberates, when they fail to lay on the listener an onus to participate in the transformation of the world. They degenerate into "mere

[14] Freire, *op. cit.,* p. 75.
[15] *Ibid.,* pp. 75-76.

words"—vocables floating harmlessly in the air—if they do not aim at or in some way illuminate faithful action. Kierkegaard once complained caustically of the "perpetual Sunday twaddle" being heard in the churches of Christendom. No doubt he had in mind this impotent use of words which have no real correlates in authentic Christian praxis.

The Hebrew term *dābār* clearly conveys the notion of "word" as something more than that which is merely spoken. In the Hebrew understanding, action is implicit in a word. A word is never merely a word. The word has a dynamic energy and power of its own. It does things as well as says things.[16] "And God said, 'Let there be light'; and there was light" (Genesis 1:3).

> "So shall my word be that goes forth from my mouth;
>   it shall not return to me empty,
> but it shall accomplish that which I purpose,
>   and prosper in the thing for which I sent it."
>
> Isaiah 55:11

In true preaching the words of a man or a woman participate in this creative power of the divine Word. They become vehicles of transforming and liberating action. This does not happen, of course, in any magical way. It is not a question of being "a wizard with words." There are preachers who are accomplished masters of such wizardry. They have the ability to mesmerize their audiences, holding them spellbound with dazzling rhetoric and verbal gymnastics. But the power they exercise over their listeners is short-lived. Within minutes or hours after the preacher has finished speaking, the words of the sermon have vanished into oblivion, with no residue except the fading memory of a flashy performance.

The only antidote for such impotent wordiness in the pulpit lies in the incarnation of the word in the flesh of human praxis. The word of the preacher acquires weight and power only when it is an integral part of the ongoing praxis of a community of liberation which combines both reflection and action. Preaching then becomes a medium through which a congregation in mission is helped to reflect on the concrete implications for action of a faithful obedience to the gospel. Preaching, understood as praxis, is part of the continuing

---

[16] For a helpful discussion of the "Word" in its biblical usages, cf. Raymond E. Brown, *The Gospel According to John (I-XII)*, The Anchor Bible (Garden City, N.Y.: Doubleday & Company, Inc., 1966), vol. 29, pp. 519-524.

dialogue of the church which moves back and forth between reflection on the meaning of the Word of God and its own liberating mission in the world.

If the tension between reflection and action is relaxed in one direction or another, something less than a liberating praxis will result. Reflection without action is empty; action without reflection is blind. Preaching that does not issue a concrete summons to obedient action is in danger of becoming innocuous verbalizing. On the other hand, preaching which fails to serve as a vehicle of theological reflection and illumination can result in sheer activism—action for action's sake—which lacks critical perspectives for guiding genuinely liberating change. Preaching begins to realize its true potential for liberation when it serves as the catalyst of dialogical reflection on real problems and issues rising out of the ministry of the laity in the world.

I am aware that the preaching model I have been recommending represents an ideal which may seem quite unrealistic to many suburban preachers. It presupposes a context for preaching which is not often found in suburban churches—that is, a situation where there is a group of people prepared to dialogue about significant issues of mission and ministry to the world. Not many of us, for example, are as fortunately situated as Gordon Cosby of the Church of the Saviour in Washington, D.C., who ministers to a unique congregation, every member of which actively participates in a mission group of some kind.[17]

The absence of such ideal conditions for engaging a congregation in the praxis of liberation should not, however, lead to a counsel of despair and resignation. There is a liberating dynamic for change in the gospel which, when faithfully proclaimed, can create new beginnings even out of the most unpromising soil. Moreover, in most congregations, there is a remnant of turned-on Christians to whom the minister can relate as natural allies in the patient and deliberate process of cultivating a community of liberation. It is with these who have a more radical vision and commitment to the Christian faith that strategizing for mission can begin and spread within the congregation. They can provide the nucleus around which a more intentional dialogical community can grow and out of which a more meaningful engagement with the issues of human liberation can develop.

[17] Cf. Gordon Cosby, *Handbook for Mission Groups* (Waco, Tex.: Word, Inc., 1975).

Such an undertaking imposes considerable demands of patience and self-restraint on a minister with a strong commitment to liberation. Quantum leaps in the liberation of a congregation are not ordinarily possible. The itch to play the prophetic role may tempt some to try to move a congregation too fast, with the result that unnecessary resistances are built up against any agenda for liberating change. The minister must be sensitive to the rhythms of a congregation's life and growth and be prepared to make realistic judgments about what the people are able to hear and to bear at a given point in their journey toward freedom. Liberation, for a congregation as well as an individual, is not possible without a process of consciousness raising, which can be very painful. But if that process is pushed at too rapid a pace, the amount of trauma experienced may rise above people's level of tolerance for pain. And they will retreat from the dialogue.

If this sounds like the cop-out of tokenism or gradualism, we need to remember that our Lord himself did not unpack for his disciples the full implications of his messianic mission all at once. He led them one step at a time into an ever-deeper understanding of what he was about. "I have yet many things to say to you, but you cannot bear them now" (John 16:12).

The wise minister will not begin with the most blatantly controversial issues to engage the congregation in dialogical action. This is not to say that he or she should avoid the taking of risks, especially when events force an issue in such a way that a choice must be made between uttering a courageous word or maintaining a faithless silence. There are times when one cannot wait for a general consensus to develop. There are times when overriding issues of Christian conscience must be addressed, and those who are ready and able to move on those issues must be supported, even at the risk of congregational conflict and schism.

As a matter of general strategy, however, it is best to begin to model an authentic liberating praxis around issues which are perceived as relatively less threatening to the majority of the congregation. The crisis of world hunger provided one such opening for dialogical action in our church. A half acre of lawn behind the parsonage became the site of a "hunger garden" where vegetables were grown and sold to church members and townspeople to raise money for world hunger projects. While this was a largely symbolic way of addressing the hunger issue, there were spin-offs from the project which provided additional opportunities for both action and reflection. A public forum with our congressman helped to focus the political dimensions of the problem and its solution. Discussions among housewives in the congregation of the dietary implications of the hunger crisis raised economic life-style questions for many.

In this action-reflection context, sermons such as "Bread and Brotherhood," "Scandal at the Lord's Table," and "Thanksgiving in a Consumer Society" were able to be heard as part of a wider dialogue going on in the church. As an attempt to articulate the imperatives of the gospel in relation to the plight of the poor and hungry of the world, the sermons contributed a theological dimension to a consciousness-raising process which was already taking place.

The Use of Liberating Images

In Freire's method of conscientization, what mediates the dialogue between teachers and students is not so much words as abstract symbols but, rather, the world as a concrete, problematic reality. Participants in the dialogue are presented with "coded" representations of concrete, existential situations encountered in the world—a picture, an article, a dramatic sketch. The purpose of these codifications is to challenge the dialoguers to critical reflection on their views of the world and their relation to it. As the dialogue proceeds, a process of decoding occurs. As they recognize themselves in the coded situations, individuals become more explicitly aware of the nature of the realities which oppress them, as well as hitherto unrealized and untested possibilities of liberating action open to them by which their situation in the world can be changed.[18]

There are striking parallels, it seems to me, between Freire's use of codified existential situations in the conscientizing process and Jesus' use of parables in preaching. Parables communicate truth not in abstract verbal formulations but through concrete images which mirror life situations with which people can readily identify. Like Freire's codifications of existential reality, parables represent situations that are sufficiently familiar to people who can immediately relate to them and recognize themselves in them. They are about such things as absentee landlords, a farmer sowing his seed, an ingrate of a son who goes out to sow his wild oats, a victim of bandits on the Jericho road who was befriended by a stranger. At the

[18] Cf. Freire, *op. cit.,* chapter 3.

same time, the parables are not so transparent that their points are self-evidently clear. They challenge the hearer to a process of critical reflection in order to decode their meaning. In the decoding process something happens to the hearer. Consciousness is raised to a new level, and new possibilities for liberating action are disclosed.

We would do well to follow Jesus' example in his parabolic approach to preaching. The fatal flaw of much contemporary preaching is its deadly abstractness. As an ex-professor, I have had to learn the hard way that impeccable logic, finely crafted arguments, and carefully balanced theological formulations do not a sermon make. Reuel Howe writes:

> Perhaps preaching has not had more power because preachers have been afraid to speak and let their message go. Instead, they try to ensure its purity by their precise theological formulations, but these forms of thought may not be appropriate for their people—with the result that the Word is not able to inform the decisions and actions of the laity.[19]

Howe suggests that the real function of the sermon is analogous to the rocket which starts orbital flight. A sermon's purpose is to "put the thought of the congregation into orbit" in such a way that the sermon is carried into the world through their lay ministries.

The power to put thought and action into orbit in this way does not come from abstract forms of speech but from concrete, arresting images which engage the whole person by stirring emotion, inciting reflection, and motivating action. In preaching, as in other forms of communication, "a picture is worth a thousand words." Effective preaching makes a continuing claim on the creative imagination. The cutting edge of a great sermon is always some liberating image which haunts the mind of the hearer long after the sermon is over, prodding it into new perceptions of the gospel, the self, and the world. The most gratifying kind of response to a sermon which a preacher can receive comes in comments like "I never saw it quite that way before," or "Your sermon made me conscious of some things about myself that I wasn't aware of." Such comments indicate that the preacher has been successful in communicating a compelling image of concrete reality with which the hearer has been able to identify and through which consciousness has been raised to a new level.

What is at stake here is not simply finding sermon illustrations to make preaching more interesting. Often illustrations are used to

[19] Howe, *op. cit.,* p. 74.

titillate and entertain or provide filler for the sermon. Such a use of illustrations for their own sake may be more diversionary than helpful. What gives the sermon liberating momentum beyond its moment of utterance is a master image which catches up in a coherent imaginative synthesis a variety of related themes to be decoded by the listener. This complex of themes reflects not only an interpretation of the meaning of the gospel but also concrete perceptions of the self and the world.

The sermon itself will begin the process of unpacking or decoding the themes implicit in its master image. Good preaching, however, will leave part of this process to the listener to complete. If it is all done for one by the preacher, nothing is left to the imagination of the hearer. In effect, he or she is barred from entrance into the dialogue. The hearer is not invited or challenged to engage in reflection and make his or her own applications of the image of truth with which he or she has been confronted. To put it another way, when the preacher leaves nothing to the imagination of the listener, the latter is robbed of the chance to speak his or her own word to the world.

Liberating preaching will stimulate rather than stifle the imagination of the listener. It will suggest, but not exhaustively define or circumscribe, reflective and actional responses which are appropriate to the message. It will plant in people's minds germinal images which, even when the sermon is over, will continue to spawn critical thought and faithful action in the context of their servanthood to the world.

The reader may be interested in examining the sample sermons in the final section of this book, with a view to identifying the overarching, controlling images which give them their coherence and which shape their basic flow of thought. In some, the image is more explicitly drawn than in others. In the case of the sermon "Jesus: The Refugee," there was a deliberate attempt to counteract the force of inauthentic images of Jesus with an image more congruent with the Gospel story. The image developed in the sermon focused in a concrete way on a number of related themes. There were certain Christological convictions about the nature and mission of Christ and his solidarity with the poor and rejected of the world. Concerning the plight of Indo-Chinese refugees, there was concrete data gleaned from a member of the congregation who was active in refugee resettlement. The theme of suburban isolation ("a society which would like to keep you out of sight and out of mind") was at least hinted at. The theme of what constitutes an appropriate way for people of faith to celebrate Christmas was also implicit in the image. No doubt, individual listeners identified additional themes as they decoded the image of Jesus, the refugee and its meaning for their lives in the contemporary situation.

As pointed out in the previous chapter, this particular sermon did, in fact, serve as a focal point for an exercise in liberating praxis which brought a refugee family into the community. "Operation Samaritan" captured the imagination not only of the congregation but the community as well. Two feature articles in the local newspaper and an editorial entitled "Room at the Inn" extended the consciousness-raising process beyond the confines of our own church. Physicians, teachers, and merchants offered their services as a ministry to the family. Here was a case where preaching helped to "put into orbit" the *diakonia* of lay people in a way which made a significant Christian witness to an entire community.

To the theological purist, this use of images to bear the weight of Christian proclamation may seem like risky business. The concrete image, to be sure, is more elusive, more vulnerable to the vagaries of subjective interpretation than the abstract idea. But if we are not willing to run the risk of allowing the idea (word) to become flesh, its liberating potential is not likely to be released into the life of the world. It is images, not ideas, which have the greatest power to move the heart and energize the will to action.

The truth of the gospel cannot, in any case, be "nailed down" in abstract propositions. It has to be "let loose" in fleshly incarnations in order to do its liberating work. To be sure, some abstract language is always essential to interpret the meaning of the Word made flesh. But abstract ways of speaking can never be a substitute for the concrete imaging of the Word in both language and life. Only through such imaging can preaching become a truly incarnational event.

A Spirituality of Liberation

Any discussion of what it takes to cultivate a community of liberation is finally incomplete without some reference to the role of Christian spirituality. "Where the Spirit of the Lord is, there is liberty" (2 Corinthians 3:17b). There can be no truly liberated and truly liberating community without sustaining roots which are sunk deeply in the life of the Spirit. As Gutiérrez puts it, "Theological categories are not enough. We need a vital attitude, all-embracing and synthesizing, informing the totality as well as every detail of our lives; we need a spirituality." [20]

What is a spirituality? In a word, it is the concrete way in which we synthesize and live out the gospel under the inspiration and dominion of the Holy Spirit. Moltmann reminds us:

> Spirituality does not only mean the inner life of devotion and prayer, cut off from the world; it is also the conduct of life in distinguishing one spirit from another, and in making decisions under the guidance of the Holy Spirit. Spirituality includes the whole of life, soul and body, individual and community, the inner life and the outward one. [21]

The church today faces a major crisis in its understanding and practice of spirituality. This crisis stems from the inability to synthesize in a unified whole the inner and the outer, the individual and the communal, the contemplative and the active dimensions of life in the Spirit. The "inner journey" too often is divorced from the "outer journey." As a result, the spiritual life of individuals and congregations is tragically fragmented and stunted, and liberation is experienced only in partial and alienated forms.

A spirituality of liberation will hold together in creative tension polarities of the spiritual life which are too often split apart—prayer and politics, contemplation and action, conversion to Christ and conversion to the neighbor. There is no intrinsic conflict between prayer and liberating politics. Indeed the devotional life of the Christian inevitably begins to suffer from unreality and triviality when it becomes insulated from the struggles for justice and liberation going on in the world. On the other hand, the activist Christian engaged in the often debilitating and frustrating struggle for social justice will soon show signs of battle fatigue and spiritual disorientation if her or his spirit is not renewed.

When a meaningful prayer life is combined with a commitment to justice, it can make the Christian more alert to potential openings for liberation created by the Spirit in the political field.

> Prayer for the Spirit makes people watchful and sensitive. It makes them vulnerable and stimulates all the powers of the imagination to perceive the coming of God in the liberation of man and to move into accord with it. This prayer therefore leads to political watchfulness, and political watchfulness leads to prayer. [22]

[20] Gustavo Gutiérrez, *A Theology of Liberation* (Maryknoll, N.Y.: Orbis Books, 1973), p. 203.
[21] Moltmann, *op. cit.,* p. 276.
[22] *Ibid.,* p. 287.

A spirituality which combines prayer and politics is obviously not suited to those who yearn for a piety which brings peace of mind and shielding from conflict. A commitment to the liberation of the oppressed in an unjust world inevitably leads us along some Via Dolorosa to a cross. Our charismatically inclined brothers and sisters who revel in their enjoyment of the gifts of the Spirit are in danger of forgetting the cross of conflict and suffering which lies at the heart of the Christian experience. The true liberation of the Spirit is impossible without a spirituality of cross bearing. The *charismata* of the Spirit and the *stigmata* of the cross go hand in hand. And where there is no evidence of the latter, the authenticity of the former is always suspect. As Bonhoeffer once said in the midst of his struggle with the oppression of Nazism, "When Christ calls a man, he bids him come and die."

This is not to deny that spiritual joy and ecstasy are marks of Christian spirituality and a liberated life-style. They are. Indeed, it can be said that the joyless uptightness of many a suburban congregation is an ominous sign of its continuing captivity to the powers of repression and the absence of the Spirit from its common life. When, however, we begin to experience some of the first fruits of the Spirit, when God's promises of a future of freedom begin to find fulfillment in concrete present liberations, we cannot help celebrating with unrestrained joy. An authentic spirituality of liberation will include the celebration of "the feast of freedom"—a joyful thanksgiving for liberations already won and a lively hope for liberations still to come.

The problem comes when we try to perpetuate and cling to our experiences of festal joy, just as Peter tried to settle down on the Mount of Transfiguration while evil spirits still held people in bondage in the valley below. A truly Christian spirituality will contain a healthy dose of eschatological tension which resists the temptation to celebrate the coming of the kingdom prematurely. Its ecstasy will be tempered by the remembrance of those who still chafe under the chains of captivity and oppression.

Spirituality cannot, then, be an escape from God's still unfinished mission of liberation in the world. Rather, it should be the dynamo which energizes us to persevere in that mission in the face of whatever opposition and frustration may come. The energizing essence of a spirituality of liberation is hope. "By his great mercy we have been born anew to a living hope through the resurrection of

Jesus Christ from the dead"(1 Peter 1:3). It is that resurrection hope, which is none other than the hope of final liberation from the last enemy of freedom, that sustains the community of faith in its continuing liberation struggles.

The spirituality of liberation which I have all too briefly sketched here is not something that can be artificially contrived and programmed. When all is said and done, it is a creation of the Spirit. Such a spirituality grows out of the sufferings and hopes of a people on their way to becoming a community of liberation. I am convinced, however, that it grows best when Christians come together in small covenant groups pledged to mutual dialogue and support. In the context of prayer, Bible study, and reflection on concrete issues of liberating praxis, a new and vital spirituality can come to birth. That spirituality is the lifeblood of the church as well as the foundation for a liberating ministry of preaching.

Part Three

Case Studies in Liberation Preaching

1

Free Indeed: Our Gospel of Liberation

TEXT: John 8:36

During our bicentennial year, we will be hearing a great deal about freedom. The rhetoric of freedom will be filling the air for some time to come. And much of it will center on our own Lexington Battle Green, as the historic events which occurred there two hundred years ago are rehearsed and their meaning for the history of American freedom is discussed and debated.

In all of this we need to be alert to the fact that freedom is one of those chameleon words in our language which tends to mean many things to many people, depending on their experience and background. It means something rather different to an old person confined to a nursing home than it does to an exuberant teenager with his own car and a generous allowance. I am sure that an unemployed black person in Roxbury has a different angle on freedom than an executive vice-president of a firm on Route 128. Let us not jump too quickly to the conclusion, then, that when we talk about America, "the land of the free and the home of the brave," we all experience and understand our American freedom in the same way.

During our upcoming Bicentennial emphasis, we need to be careful that we are not seduced by patriotic sloganeering into entertaining notions of freedom which are difficult to square with the gospel of Christ. That gospel is, above all, I'm convinced, a gospel of liberation. As we have been reminded again by our text, "If the Son makes you free, you will be free indeed." You will be really free!

A friend of mine from Germany said in a sermon not long ago, "The impression that a Christian man is a free man who disseminates liberation is seldom publicly generated." How tragically true that is! But how out of keeping with the gospel! For if the gospel says anything to us, it says that Christ has come to set us free—to make us free indeed!

The freedom story began, of course, before Jesus. Read the history of the people of Israel, and you read the story of a people's "stride towards freedom." The central symbol of that story was the Exodus—the symbol of emancipation from every oppressive power. The central actor in that story was Jahweh—the Liberator of his people—indeed, the source and power of human liberation itself.

Then, in the fullness of time, Jesus came to "proclaim release to the captives . . . to set at liberty those who are oppressed" (Luke 4:18b). Under the impact of his life and death and resurrection, the church was born as the community of the liberated people of God "called," as Paul said, "to freedom." In his letters to the churches, Paul again and again grew ecstatic about the message of liberation. "Where the Spirit of the Lord is, there is freedom" (2 Corinthians 3:17b). "For freedom Christ has set us free; stand fast therefore, and do not submit again to a yoke of slavery" (Galatians 5:1). You can hear his heart dancing and exulting at the thought of it. The Son had made him free—really free!

But what does it mean to be really free? It is possible for us to labor under the illusion that we are free when, in fact, we are in the deepest kind of bondage. As Goethe once said, "No one is more of a slave than he who thinks himself free without being so." This was certainly the case with the Jewish audience to whom Jesus addressed the words of our text. When he said to them, "You will know the truth, and the truth will make you free," their pride resisted the thought that they, of all people, needed liberation. "We are descendants of Abraham, and have never been in bondage to anyone," they declared heatedly. "What do you mean by saying, 'You will be made free'?" (See John 8:32-34.)

Jesus' response was to go directly to the root of their bondage. "Truly, truly, I say to you, every one who commits sin is a slave to sin." The underlying cause of all slavery and oppression, Jesus says, in effect, is sin. But what is sin? Unless we have a way of bringing that three-letter word down out of the clouds of generality and anchoring it in our experience, we have not gotten very far toward understanding the source of our unfreedom.

Let me take a stab at clarifying what sin means. Biblically understood, sin is not a matter of violating a list of "no-no's" enshrined in a law book. If it were, liberation from sin would be a very nonliberating thing, indeed. For then we would be slaves to the law, which was precisely the problem Jesus saw in the Pharisees. No! Sin is the way we anxious and insecure human beings try to establish our security and identity on our own terms, usually at the expense of others.

There are various strategies we employ to try to guarantee our own security and significance. Sometimes we make a fetish out of our material possessions and bow down to the idols of our status symbols—all to make us feel more important in the scheme of things. Sometimes we put other people down—whether blacks, or women, or lazy welfare recipients—in order to give our fragile, threatened egos a boost. Or we may find ways of fencing other people out of our exclusive preserve in order to maintain the myth of our own superiority. Viewed in this way, it is not hard to see how sin is a form of bondage which makes oppressors of us all, even though, like the Jews to whom Jesus spoke, we may be the last ones to be aware of it.

How does Jesus deliver us from this kind of bondage? How does the Son really make us free? He does so by bringing home to us the affirming, accepting love of God with such force and power that the anxiety which feeds our sin is laid to rest. In the love of Jesus which went all the way to the cross for us, we are grasped by the unconditional love of God which accepts us and gives us the courage to accept ourselves.

Because of that love, we do not have to contrive our own security and prove our own importance. Because we are secure in the love of God and important in his sight, there is no longer any need for us to resort to desperate mechanisms to bolster our collapsing egos to the hurt and detriment of others. We no longer have to manipulate things and persons to insure our own security from without; for deep within we have a wonderfully freeing sense of security which is God's gift to us in Christ. We are free indeed!

What does a person's life look like who has entered in this way into "the glorious liberty of the sons of God"? The resignation of William Sloane Coffin from the chaplaincy of Yale, after seventeen years of service in that institution, gives us some clues. In his resignation statement he acknowledged that New Haven had become for him a "safe haven." He said that he was delighted that the future is unsure. "That's the way it should be. Growth demands willingness to relinquish one's proficiencies. So I want to become more vulnerable, or as the old Pietist phrase goes, 'to let go and let God.'"

In editorializing on the event, the *Boston Globe* made a discerning observation: "What a far cry all this is from the current fetish of grabbing all one can for one's own security and of not caring a whit about what happens to the rest of mankind!"

Would that we had more models of liberated Christians like that—men and women who are the true sons and daughters of Abraham—free men and women who disseminate liberation wherever they go! People who want to make themselves more vulnerable—because God in Christ has made himself utterly vulnerable for us!

Make no mistake about it! If the Son has really made you free, it will show up in the totality of your life-style. The freedom which is the gift of Christ is not some partial, inward, merely spiritual thing. It is a lot more even than what we Baptists used to call "soul-liberty." It encompasses the "outer man" as well as the "inner man." Christ is still at work in the world as the Great Emancipator, striking the shackles from people's bodies and minds, as well as their souls. Every freedom movement which delivers men and women from prisons of physical poverty, social inferiority, and mental and spiritual bondage bears his name—whether publicly or anonymously. And he calls you and me to be a part of that ongoing freeing work.

As we gather around the Lord's table this morning, may his matchless love symbolized in the bread and wine make you free indeed! May it free you up to join in the fellowship of the liberating Christ! May it move you to share in the freeing-up action that is going on in the world today in his name and for his sake!

2

On Being a Man

TEXT: Philippians 2:5-8; Mark 10:42-45

This morning I want to continue a discussion of an area of concern which I opened up on Mother's Day in a sermon "Free to Be." The burden of my message at that time was to suggest that women are freed by the gospel from all inhibiting stereotypes which prevent them from realizing the fullness of their humanity.

Father's Day may be an appropriate time to make a similar point with respect to men. While we hear a great deal about women's liberation today, I believe there are important ways in which men need to be liberated as well. Men in our culture are victimized by certain images of themselves, certain notions of what it takes really to be a man, which add up to a form of bondage. Distorted images of masculinity drive men compulsively to "prove their manhood" in ways which take a terrible toll in frustration and destructiveness. These images imply, moreover, an ideal of manhood which is utterly inconsistent with what we know of the manhood of Jesus Christ and the picture of the new humanity which he came to pioneer in the world.

Let's look at some of these masculine images this morning and reflect a little on what they do to us. We find them mirrored in the life-style of our cultural heroes—the men who inspire the admiration of other men. We say, "He is a man's man." And we point to the John Waynes, the Joe Namaths, the Henry Kissingers, the General

Pattons. These are the male identity models which provide the clues for hosts of middle-class men as to what it means to be a "real man." These are the kind of men the Archie Bunkers of this world look up to. And let's not kid ourselves. There's a little of Archie in all of us. That's why he continues to repel and fascinate us year after year on television.

A "real man," according to the popular mythology, is a "self-made man." He is the very picture of self-sufficiency and self-reliance. He prides himself on making it through life on his own, without having to acknowledge dependence on anyone but himself. He sees the world as a threatening jungle or an obstacle course against which to pit his manhood and prove his superior strength. If you are a real man, you can make it to the top by dint of hard work and your own ingenuity and resourcefulness. And your reward is the opportunity to exercise power over others, to make decisions for others, and to command their respect and approval by your superior ability and status.

Archie Bunker mirrors beautifully this image of masculine self-sufficiency and superiority in one of his exchanges with Mike in an "All in the Family" episode. "I've been making my way in this world for a long time, sonny boy," he proclaims proudly, "and one thing I know—a man better watch out for number one. It's the survival of the fittest!" How very much like old Adam Archie is! Both of them idolators! Both of them trying to play God! Both of them out to prove they are somebody by denying their creaturely limitations, their dependence on others and on God!

The problem is that this business of playing God is very difficult to bring off. When Adam tried it, it led to a strange new kind of self-consciousness. For the first time, he and Eve experienced shame. That shame stemmed from a dawning awareness that they had violated God's order of things by trying to assume godlike powers themselves. Not able to live with this awareness, they tried to cover up—to hide themselves from one another and from God. As the Bible describes it poetically, "Then the eyes of both were opened, and they knew that they were naked; and they sewed fig leaves together and made themselves aprons" (Genesis 3:7).

That same kind of cover-up operation has been going on ever since—all the way from Eden to Watergate. It is especially necessary for men who live by the myth of male self-sufficiency and supremacy. If your male self-image requires you to be strong and independent, then you have to hide from others and from yourself any sign of weakness, any feeling of inadequacy, any suggestion of vulnerability. And if your inadequacy is somehow found out, it is an intolerable threat to your masculine ego. Then you have to resort to even more desperate extremes to prove your manhood.

That happened to Archie when he discovered that Edith had been letting him win at Monopoly. When the cat is out of the bag, Edith says, "Well, Archie, I thought it would make you feel better if I let you win." At that point, Archie explodes: "Let me win? That'll be the day when I can't win without you letting me win. You spoiled the whole thing. From now on if you want to do something together, do it by yourself!"

How is that for an updated version of the old apron story of Genesis? Hiding the truth from ourselves so that we can preserve the myth of our self-sufficiency and superiority! Pathetically trying to play God!

This need to play God is fueled in our society by a compulsive masculinity which drives men to prove how tough and aggressive and competitive they can be. It is this image of masculinity that drives men unmercifully in their work—either to beat out the competition in business, or get ahead of someone else on the corporate executive ladder, or provide an ever higher material standard of living for their families. Such pressures can dehumanize a man to the point where his work defines and circumscribes his whole existence. He has no time or energy left over to be a father, or a husband, or just himself—the unique individual he is capable of being. For all his dreams of making it big, he runs the risk of ending up like Willie Loman in Arthur Miller's play *Death of a Salesman*—lonely, friendless, dying as a little man who, in the words of his son, "never knew who he was."

Not only are false masculine images dehumanizing for the man who is hung up on them, but they are also positively dangerous to anyone else who may get in his way. The game of "playing God" involves not only "operation cover-up" but "operation put-down" as well. A threatened masculine ego can feel secure only by putting someone else down. And the more insecure the ego, the more aggressive and violent is the put-down. It is because Archie Bunker is so insecure in his own manhood that he has to people the earth with wops, and gooks, and kikes, and niggers—subhuman projections of his imagination on whom he can spew out his contempt in a vain effort to bolster his own fragile ego.

What a way to prove your manhood! And yet we do it all the time. We reward our presidents in the popularity polls when they demonstrate their manhood and ours by a "tough guy" stance in international relations, whatever the cost in innocent blood. We eulogize violence and war on our TV screens and in real life as an exercise of the so-called "manly" virtues.

Sometimes we men engage in "operation put-down" in a less violent, but equally dehumanizing, way with our wives and children. Again, Archie is a perfect mirror in which we can see ourselves. Whenever Edith tries to speak up and assert her individuality, or whenever she departs in any way from the mold he has put her in, he puts her down with the words: "Stifle yourself." Edith has to be turned into a "dingbat"—a slightly less than human being—if Archie's feeling of male superiority is to remain intact. Many of us may do it with more subtlety than Archie, but for those on the receiving end, the put-down is nonetheless real.

By now it should be evident how dehumanizing are the images of masculinity of which I have been speaking this morning. To be liberated from their oppressive power, we will have to start taking our cues, not from John Wayne, but from Jesus Christ. In him is imaged for us not only true God but true humanity as well. And in the form of his humanity, as described by Paul in Philippians 2:5-8, we find the liberating antidote for the Archie Bunker ideal of what it means to be a man. "Have this mind among yourselves," says Paul, "which is yours in Christ Jesus, who, though he was in the form of God, did not count equality with God a thing to be grasped, but emptied himself, taking the form of a servant, being born in the likeness of men. And being found in human form he humbled himself and became obedient unto death, even death on a cross."

Note the striking contrasts between the form of Jesus' manhood and the images of manhood which our society eulogizes. Not domination, but servanthood; not ego-inflation, but self-emptying; not invulnerability, but vulnerability; not success, but suffering for others; not grasping for godlike power, but strength made perfect in weakness. Here was a real man—"the strong son of God." But his strength was not the pseudo-strength of an Archie Bunker—a facade to hide an insecure and frightened ego. It was the strength of an infinite tenderness and compassion, a strength that could afford to weep for the sins and sorrows of men and women.

In the tenth chapter of Mark, there is a remarkable incident in which something very much like the Archie Bunker syndrome raises its ugly head among the disciples. James and John came to Jesus asking him for a favor. "Grant us the right to sit in state with you, one at your right and the other at your left." A little like Archie enthroned on his living room chair! When the other disciples heard that the two brothers had tried to get the edge on them in a bid for preferential status, they were indignant, for they had ambitions to make it to the top, too.

Jesus took the occasion to call them aside and share with them his radically new vision of how to be a man among men. "You know that in the world the recognized rulers lord it over their subjects, and their great men make them feel the weight of authority. That is not the way with you; among you, whoever wants to be great must be your servant, and whoever wants to be first must be the willing slave of all. For even the Son of Man did not come to be served but to serve, and to give up his life as a ransom for many." (See Mark 10:35-45, NEB.)

Jesus is saying that to be a real man in God's way of ordering human relationships, we have to have done, once and for all, with all notions of domination, superiority, and lording it over others. The truly liberated man is one who is not above playing the servant role. He does not have to prove his manhood by either the cover-up or the put-down. For his manhood is secure and his worth is established, not because of anything he has done, but because God has accepted him unconditionally in Jesus Christ.

One of the greatest things that can happen to a man is to be liberated by the grace of God from the dehumanizing bondage of having to prove his own manhood. That is the gift of the gospel to every man here this morning. I challenge you to accept that gift and begin to live and act like a free man.

3

Our Stewardship of the Earth: Ecology and Faith

TEXT: Psalm 24:1; Genesis 2:15

This is the third sermon I have preached in recent weeks on the theme of stewardship. But now I hope you have begun to get hold of the idea that stewardship is a much broader concept than pledging or giving to the church. Stewardship, in the biblical view, has to do with a total life-style. It is a matter of our responsibility and responsiveness to God in relation to his total entrustments to us.

The notion of stewardship presupposes that we are called to have "a piece of the action" in God's great ventures of creation and redemption. It assumes that, as Paul put it, we are not our own, but are "bought with a price" (1 Corinthians 6:20a). It implies, moreover, that we don't have any exclusive property rights to anything we possess. We are responsible to God for the way we use our talent, our time, our influence, our opportunities, our material possessions. We are accountable to him for the way we care for the Good News of the gospel, as well as for the way we care for persons and their potential.

Today I want to talk for a while about our accountability to God for the care of the earth. This is a strand in the biblical idea of stewardship which is particularly important for us to emphasize today. For we are living at a time when the earth is an endangered planet in a way in which it has never been throughout its long history. There has, perhaps, never been a generation before ours when people had such a widespread sense of the earth's mortality. No longer do we automatically assume, as other generations did before us, that this fair earth of ours will go on and on forever. Indeed, there are increasing numbers of doomsayers among the scientists who are prepared to predict rather imminent ecological disaster for our planet unless we quickly and drastically mend our ways.

In such a crisis, the time is long overdue when Christians should begin to develop an ecological conscience to go along with their social conscience. Vital faith and sound ecology do go together, I am convinced, and stewardship is the bridge which links them.

An adequate understanding of what is involved in our stewardship of the earth must begin with the recognition that "the earth is the Lord's." In the words of the Twenty-fourth Psalm, "The earth is the Lord's and all that is in it, the world and those who dwell therein" (v. 1, NEB). Unless we get our heads and our hearts straight about that fundamental axiom, nothing else we say about stewardship is going to make much sense. Let's make sure we are clear about who is in charge here! Let's not try to kid ourselves about who owns the farm! "The earth is *the Lord's* and all that is in it." A pretty sweeping claim to ownership title, don't you think? He's got *the whole world* in his hands. You would think that would be enough to settle the matter.

But it doesn't really. Along come the likes of you and me with the audacity to assert our property rights over our little bit of earth. Here is a creature called "man" with the arrogance to assume that the world is his oyster to do with as he wills. And he sets out to exploit it for his own advantage and profit.

Man who, according to the psalmist, was created a "little less than God" (Psalm 8:5), in fact tries to play God in his relation to nature. He rapes and pillages the earth in the name of profit and progress. He plunders its dwindling resources to satisfy his insatiable appetite for more and more consumer goods. He poisons its skies and seas with pollutants which are the by-products of that same greed. And, in the ultimate abuse of his godlike power, he threatens to blow up his own home—spaceship earth—with death-dealing weapons aimed at his fellow-humans with whom he competes for space and power and food.

What a tragic reversal of God's plan for his creation! Unfortunately, there has been a good deal of misunderstanding and confusion about what the Bible really teaches about the relationship which should exist between humans and nature. There have been those who have seen that relationship solely in terms of domination and control. "Fill the earth and subdue it," God said to Adam in the Genesis story of creation; "have dominion over every living thing" (see Genesis 1:28). Taken by itself, that could be understood as a blank check for humanity to use and abuse nature any way it wanted. Man is in charge here, God having "put all things under his feet" (Psalm 8:6b). There has been no shortage of folks ready to proceed as if that were the last and only word about humanity's proper relationship to nature.

Fortunately, it is not. One day Robert Louis Stevenson came upon a man beating a dog. Stevenson, always a great lover of nature, tried to stop him. The owner objected. "It's not your dog," he shouted. "No," Stevenson answered, "it's God's dog, and I'm here to protect it."

That anecdote helps a lot to restore the balance which we find in the biblical understanding of our place in the scheme of things. Humanity was created, to be sure, to be *over nature* but also *under God*. And that makes a world of difference. For it means that human beings are called to be stewards, custodians of God's creation, caretakers of the earth. That means we have no right to abuse nature—whether it be a dog, or the mountains of Appalachia, or the biosphere which covers and protects the earth. The earth is not ours to do with as we will. The earth is the Lord's and we are his stand-ins to protect it and manage it for the welfare of all of God's creatures.

In Genesis 2:15, we read that "the Lord God took the man and put him in the garden of Eden to till it and keep it," or, as *The Jerusalem Bible* translates it, "to cultivate and take care of it." There is the nub of it as far as our stewardship of the earth is concerned. Eden still stands as the symbol of what God intended for the whole earth—a loving cooperation between God and humanity and nature in which humanity is nature's caretaker rather than its violator and rapist.

Nature needs much more tender loving care than we have been giving her of late, in order to maintain the delicate ecological balances which spell the difference between life and death on our planet. We have been acting as if we had a blank check on the environmental bank, and we haven't. Our habits of conspicuous consumption have been using up at an alarming rate the nonrenewable natural resources of the earth. Did you know, for example, that Americans who constitute only 6 percent of the world's population consume 50 percent of the world's resources? The time is rapidly approaching when nature is going to start sending us back the message: "Your account on this bank is overdrawn. Checks will no longer be honored because of insufficient funds."

On the basis of what I have been saying this morning, surely we must conclude that faith and a keen sense of our stewardship under God cannot help but generate ecological sensitivity and concern. Christians, of all people, should be "friends of the earth." Let us remember it wasn't just us whom God loved. God so loved the world. And all of nature, as Paul reminds us in Romans 8, awaits with us the day of full redemption and liberation.

It is one thing to affirm all of this as our faith. It is another thing, however, to find practical ways of making a difference in the ecological crisis that faces us. It is easy for us to be so intimidated by the magnitude and complexity of the problem that we just throw up our hands in futility. What can an ordinary person like me do about something as overwhelming as the ecological crisis?

Let me close with a couple of suggestions of things that each of us can do to make a difference. First, we can put high on our checklist for deciding on candidates and issues in the upcoming election the matter of environmental concern. I cannot tell you how to vote. But I have no hesitation at all in urging you, as an expression of your Christian faith, to make your vote count as a good friend and steward of the earth. Christians need to be in the vanguard today of those who are about the business of creating a new set of values in our country. This may sometimes lead to some difficult choices. Sometimes we may have to choose, for example, between good ecology and bad business. When that happens, we need to be willing to signal our leaders that we are in favor of improving our environment even at the expense of more modest profits and smaller returns on our investments.

There is another area in which we can make a difference. That is in our personal and family life-style. As I said in the beginning, stewardship is largely a question of life-style. There is simply no way we can begin to call a halt to the rape of the earth and feed the hungry of the world until you and I begin to mean business about embracing a simpler life-style, until we start resisting the pressures toward higher and higher levels of consumption.

It may sound subversive to our American way of life—and I suppose, in a way, it is. But I believe that it is time for people of religious convictions to band together to resist the ideology of consumerism which, more than anything else, is pushing our endangered earth to the brink of disaster. At the very least, we need to be putting to ourselves some hard questions: Is it really necessary for our sense of self-importance that we stay in the rat race to keep up with the Joneses? Do we really need the latest model or fashion, or won't last year's or the year's before do just as well? Are our lives really so empty, so bereft of meaning, that we have to turn to the latest luxury gadgets and technological toys to relieve our boredom? These are questions which should answer themselves if you have really bought into the Christian faith and made it the dynamic of your daily life-style.

You see, there is really more at stake here than the survival of a home for the human family. That surely is important, particularly for our children and our children's children. But more immediately important for you now is the question of the health of your own soul—the values by which you live, the kind of goods on which you stake your life. "For what is a man profited," Jesus warned, "if he shall gain the whole world, and lose his own soul?" (Matthew 16:26*a*, KJV).

Strangely enough, we cannot separate our stewardship of the earth from the salvation of our souls. When God gets us into a right relationship with himself, he also transforms our relationship with nature—from being nature's predators to becoming nature's caretakers—faithful stewards of the earth. May it be so with each of us.

4

Jesus:
The Refugee

TEXT: Matthew 2:13-21

The Christmas story is a rich tapestry of vivid images and symbols which have captured the imagination of men and women through the centuries—the star of Bethlehem, the angelic chorus on the Judean hillside, the Magi and shepherds bringing their homage to a cherubic infant peacefully cradled in a manger. All of this is what pageants are made of. Musicians, poets, artists, preachers have all taken these simple and eloquent images from the Gospels and wrought their own kind of magic with them in the hearts and minds of people in every generation.

Recently Musak and the department store executives have gotten into the act and given their macabre twist to the symbols of Christmas. In their hands, the baby Jesus becomes a convenient public relations image to sell everything from booze to electronic ball games. I must say that it jars my Christian sensitivities to hear "Joy to the World, the Lord Is Come" sung in Burlington Mall to the tinkling of the cash registers. That strikes me as being as far from the true reality of Christmas as did the recorded voice of Bing Crosby crooning "I'm Dreaming of a White Christmas" during our visit to the Church of the Annunciation in Nazareth a year ago.

The fact is that our images of Christmas have become so synthetic and plastic that one begins to doubt how much of the true meaning of Christmas they can carry any longer. We are in desperate need, I believe, of an image of Jesus which will rescue him from commercial exploitation and banality and put us in touch again with the biblical realities of his birth. This morning I want to suggest to you just such an image—the image of Jesus the Refugee.

Perhaps you have never thought of it that way before—I confess that it hit me only recently—that Jesus began his earthly career as a political refugee. He was a homeless waif from the beginning—making his entrance into the world, not in the inviting warmth of the Bethlehem Hilton, but in a cold and drafty cattle stall.

But even that rude shelter was not to be his for long. When Herod heard from the wise men about a baby born to be a king, he began at once to concoct a ruthless scheme to get rid of any such pretender to his throne. The slaughter of the innocents was the bloody outcome of his plan—every child of two years and under slain by the sword. It was this impending massacre which made Jesus and his parents refugees—victims of the insecurity of power which cannot tolerate any threat of opposition, real or imagined.

The slaughter of the innocents and the flight of the holy family to Egypt are harsh and haunting images which are also part and parcel of the Christmas story. No doubt it is because of their very harshness that they have customarily been excluded from the Nativity pageantry. Christmas is not a time when we want to listen to Rachel weeping for her children, refusing to be consoled. And the reality of the refugee is not one which is comfortable at a time when we are filling our living rooms with expensive gifts for one another.

Still, Jesus the Refugee cannot be expunged from the record—then or now. Without this dimension of the Nativity story, we miss the full meaning of the incarnation. It isn't enough to say that God became incarnate in human form. We must ask what kind of role he played in human life. It wasn't just a happenstance that the Son of God was not born the son of the proprietor of the Bethlehem Hilton, or, for that matter, a prince in Herod's palace. The drama of salvation called for a different part from that for Jesus to play. The script called for one who would be an outsider. It called for a son of man who had nowhere to lay his head, even though the foxes had holes and the birds of the air their nests. It called for one who was "despised and rejected by men; a man of sorrows, and acquainted with grief" (Isaiah 53:3a). It called for someone who was persona non grata among his own people, who "came unto his own, and his own received him not" (John 1:11, KJV).

Yes, Jesus was a refugee. And he is a refugee still. Why? Because the refugee represents the deepest pathos and extremity of human need to which the love of God can reach. If you are a refugee, you are among those who are the unwanted of the world, the rejects of a society which would like to keep you out of sight and out of mind. The refugee, like the rest of the "invisible poor," is kept at a distance, in a remote camp somewhere, where he is unable to disturb the slumbering conscience of the rest of us.

But no one who truly believes in the Christmas message that God was in Christ reconciling the world unto himself can reject the refugee without being in danger of rejecting Christ himself. For the image of Jesus the Refugee proclaims that it is precisely among the homeless and unwanted of the world that the love of God dwells in its incarnate form. Any doubt on that point is surely dispelled by Jesus' parable of the last judgment. In that parable Jesus identifies himself unreservedly with the plight of the hungry, the stranger, the naked, the sick, and the imprisoned. Insensitivity to their suffering is tantamount to a rejection of Christ himself. "As you did it not to one of the least of these, you did it not to me" (Matthew 25:45b).

Meanwhile, the slaughter of the innocents still goes on. Rachel still weeps unconsolably for her children. Just a few days ago it was reported that twenty-six Cambodian refugees, forcibly repatriated across the Thailand border as national security risks, were beheaded on their return home—men, women, and children alike. In the squalid refugee camps of Thailand, seventy-seven thousand still huddle hopelessly with no one to take them in, with food rations now cut off for all children under twelve. Meanwhile, an estimated one thousand refugees have been trying to survive in small boats off the coast of Vietnam. All part of the ongoing legacy of a cruel war we would like to forget.

And where is Jesus in all of this heartbreaking scene? No doubt with his fellow-refugees, making their homelessness his home! And Jesus will continue to be a refugee till the end of time, as long as we shut his brothers and sisters out of our homes and hearts.

There is a lovely child's legend about Jesus the Refugee with which I want to conclude. When Joseph and Mary and Jesus were on their way to Egypt, the story runs, as the evening came they grew weary and sought refuge in a cave. It was very cold—so cold, in fact, that the ground was white with hoarfrost. A little spider saw the baby Jesus, and he wished so much that he could do something for him to keep him warm. He decided to do the only thing he could do—to spin his web across the entrance of the cave, to make a kind of curtain. It happened that a detachment of Herod's soldiers came along that night, seeking for children to kill to carry out Herod's bloodthirsty orders. When they came to the cave, they were about to burst in and search it when their captain noticed the spider's web. It was covered with the white hoarfrost and stretched right across the entrance of the cave. He concluded that no one could possibly be in the cave, or they would have torn the spider's web. So the soldiers passed on and left the holy family in peace. And that, so they say, is why to this day we put tinsel on our Christmas trees; for the glittering tinsel streamers stand for the spider's web, white with hoarfrost, which kept the little refugee Christ-child safe in the cave on his way to Egypt.

I hope you will remember that beautiful story as you hang the tinsel on your tree this Christmas. But more than that, I hope that together we may be able to find ways of weaving a web of protection for some of Jesus' fellow-refugees. That might be through sponsoring a refugee family. It might be through exercising political influence to extend our nation's program of refugee resettlement which has virtually ground to a halt. Whatever the specific nature of our response, Jesus will be knocking at our door this Christmas, perhaps in a way more poignant than he has ever done before. If we are going to have him as our Christmas guest, we may have to make room for someone else, too—the one whom he holds by the hand, dressed in the thin and tattered garments of a refugee.

I hope you will be ready this Christmas to say to him in the words that we will now sing together,

> O come to my heart, Lord Jesus!
> There is room in my heart for Thee.

5

The God Who Won't Give Up on Us

Text: Luke 15:1-10

At first blush, these parables of the lost sheep and the lost coin may not strike you as having much to do with Advent. But take a second look, and I think you will find that they come close to the heart of what this season is all about. In fact, they distill the very essence of the Good News that Jesus' coming into our world represents. They tell us simply that "the Son of Man came to seek and to save the lost" (Luke 19:10). They tell us of a rescue mission set in motion by a God who refuses to give up on us, however far we may have strayed from his purposes.

As in most of his parables, Jesus was here addressing a very definite situation with a specific object in mind. He had been spending a lot of time with people who were widely regarded as being beyond the pale of respectable society—even to the point of having table fellowship with them. These were the folks whom the religious leaders had written off as sinners—not because of any flagrant immorality—but because their work kept them from observing the petty ritual details of the law. One day, as they were gathered around eagerly drinking in his teaching, Jesus overheard some scribes and Pharisees at the edge of the crowd muttering complaints about his habit of fraternizing with common sinners.

Jesus seized the occasion to tell these stories. One was about a shepherd who, on gathering his flock into the sheepfold for the night, found that one was missing. Not content to lose even one out of a hundred, he went out into the blackness of the night and searched for that one lost sheep until he found it. And finding it, he hoisted it on his shoulders and brought it home to the safety of the fold. The other story was about a woman who, having lost a precious coin, searched carefully every corner of her house until she found it. And when she found it, she called in her neighbors to help her celebrate the joy of her find.

Even the proud Pharisees should have gotten the point loud and clear. God is like that good shepherd and that persistent woman. He doesn't give up on a single one of us. Lost though we may be, he will never abandon us to our lostness. However far we may have wandered into the wilderness of alienation from his love, he is like that shepherd—he keeps on looking for us, seeking us out until he finds us. However much we may have allowed our true selves to be covered over with the accumulated dirt and debris of our sins and failures and mistakes, he is like that woman—persistently searching through the clutter of our lives till he finds us. Others may have long since given up on us. We may have given up on ourselves. But not so God! We are too precious in his sight for him to give up on a solitary one of us.

If Advent says anything, it says this—the God and Father of our Lord Jesus Christ is a patient, persistent seeker of lost men and women. He is not ready to give up on his world. He is not ready to give up on you and me. That is why again this Christmastime we can celebrate the Good News that he has sent his Son to find us and bring us home.

That is news that may seem to you just too good to be true. If life has somehow gotten away from you and you feel at sixes and sevens with yourself, you may be inclined to agree with Thomas Carlyle who, in a dark mood, complained that "God sits in his heaven and does nothing." But Advent gives the lie to that. Through his life and death, Jesus testifies to a God who, far from being unfeeling and aloof, cares enough about us to make himself fully present to us in our suffering, estrangement, and sin. He is none other than Emmanuel—God with us. His is a love which broods over us and weeps for us. His heart goes out to us and is broken for us. Indeed, his very being is threatened and diminished as long as one of us is lost to him.

How marvelously different this God is from the one we sometimes try to fashion in our own image! Often that god of our own making is more like a celestial scorekeeper who chalks up the rights and wrongs of our lives to see if we have measured up—or like a divine calculator whose infallible memory bank records our good and evil deeds and gives us a printout to tell us whether we are in the red or the black.

In some ways, I suppose, that kind of God is more comfortable to live with. At least the Pharisees thought so. With that kind of God running the show, you can neatly classify and separate the righteous from the sinners, the deserving from the undeserving, those who have made it from those who haven't. Then, at least, you know whose company to keep and from whom to keep your distance. If you are a Pharisee and know you have made it, then you can feel downright comfortable with such a God.

But what if you are a sinner, and you don't need anyone to tell you that you are? What if you are lost, and no one knows it better than you? Ah, then, my friend, is when you need the God of the Advent, the God whom Jesus came to represent and reveal! No wonder it was the sinners, the outcasts, and the lost who flocked to Jesus! For he told them of a God who valued each of them so much that he would never give them up for lost. He was prepared to go to any lengths, to expose himself to any human condition, in order to gather them and heal them and make them whole. "The Son of Man came to seek and to save those who are lost."

There is a story about a problem foster child who migrated from home to home, from one institution to another. He was so incorrigible that no one could put up with him for very long. As might be expected, after so many rejections he became increasingly hostile and violent. Finally, he was accepted by a particularly understanding couple. Within an hour of his arrival in their home, he had torn the place apart. The living room was a shambles; the bedrooms looked as if a tornado had just passed through. When the tantrum was finally over, his new father sat the boy down and said to him quietly but firmly: "No matter what you do, we will never let you go." That was the first time the boy had ever heard anything like that. His whole life had been a litany of "If you are good, we will keep you. If you behave yourself, you can stay. If you obey us, you can be our child." No one had ever told him, "We will never let you go. We will never give up on you."

That is exactly what Jesus is telling us through these parables. "I will never let you go. I will never give you up for lost." And the wonderful thing about it is that there are no conditions that we have to meet. We don't have to come crawling to make amends. God doesn't demand that we shape up or ship out. He isn't in the business of keeping moral scorecards and striking balance sheets. The only trip he lays on us is a love that will not let us go, a love that keeps searching us out and calling us home.

Can you imagine a God like that? In the movie *Oh, God* there are many gems of theological insight. To me, one of the most priceless comes at the end of the courtroom scene where George Burns, in the role of "God," has been doing his best to persuade the judge that he is really God in human form. As he walks to the door of the courtroom and suddenly disappears, his voice is heard coming back with the words, "If you have trouble believing in me, it may help you to know that I believe in you."

That, too, is part of the Advent message. God believes in you. And because he believes in you, he is not going to give up on you easily. It is so easy for us to despair of ourselves and of one another. If we are ever going to be able to hope again, our hope will have to be grounded in God's hope for us.

But this is precisely what the Good News of Advent announces— that God believes in us and he has hope for us. He has planted his own image in our hearts, and he doesn't mean for it to be lost or destroyed. He knows that in the dark recesses of our hearts, buried perhaps beneath the dirty residue of years of failure and neglect, there is a shiny coin waiting to be found. There is a possibility for good that we may have long since despaired of realizing. As an old gospel hymn puts it so well:

> Down in the human heart, Crushed by the tempter,
> Feelings lie buried that grace can restore;
> Touched by a loving heart, Wakened by kindness,
> Chords that are broken will vibrate once more.[1]

Yes, God does believe in you! And because of that, he won't give up on you—he won't let you go. Such amazing grace can find you wherever you are. It can stir something in you that you yourself may have forgotten was there. And the chords of your life can vibrate again to the music of his undying love.

Music! That's the way our stories end—with music and dancing and unrestrained joy! The search has been successful. The lost has

[1] Fanny J. Crosby, "Rescue the Perishing."

been found. The shepherd has found his sheep. The woman has found her coin. God has found his man or his woman or his people. "There is joy among the angels of God over one sinner who repents" (Luke 15:10, NEB).

Imagine that! It takes only one person who decides to give up her futile efforts to find her own way, and begins to follow Christ's way, to set the choirs of heaven to singing. It takes only one person like you, like me, to quit trying to lift himself by his own bootstraps and, like the sheep, to allow himself to be lifted on the shoulders of the shepherd and carried home. It takes only one person like that to make God's heart dance for joy.

Let us remember, then, the God who won't give up on us until we have given in to him—the God who makes our hearts restless till they find their rest in him. We would really have something to celebrate this Christmas if, accepting the glad fact that God believes in us, we started really to believe in one another and ourselves. What a great thing it would be if the faith of this season, that God will never give up on us, inspired in us the determination not to give up on one another! That is my prayer, my hope for us all at this Christmas time.